Dark Valley Porter

Chloe Taylor

Printed in the United States of America
First Printing, 2024
ISBN: 9798322339922

Edited by Ashly Wallace
Penning for Your Thoughts Editing

*This book is dedicated to both of my parents,
for always encouraging me to chase my
dreams, and ensuring that I knew anything
was possible as long as I believed.*

*Thank you, daddy,
I'll be running when the sand runs out*

*Mama,
I love you to the moon and back always*
☾

Contents

Content Warnings

This book contains serious topics of child abuse and neglect.

Please protect your mental health.

For a full list of trigger warnings please go to
www.writtenbychloe.com

Dark Valley Porter Playlist

Created by Chloe Taylor

Playlist Guide

Stella's songs
Inside Her Head
Breathe Me
Panic Room
RIP 2 My Youth

Kaleb's song
Quick intimacy

Kaleb/Stella songs
Nervous
Can You Hold Me
To Build a Home
13 Beaches

Porter's song
Already Gone

Judith's songs
You're somebody else
Gone

Book theme songs
Lovely
Mansion
Quick intimacy

I listened to Gone on repeat when writing chapter twenty-one and To Build a
Home on repeat when writing the epilogue and Already Gone.

Prologue

There's red. Red, orange, white, and it's hot, so hot. I feel a bead of sweat roll down my face and over my scar. I cough from the smoke. I can't move from where I sit; my body won't budge.

I'm stuck.

Sitting in the grass, pain flooding my body, and barely conscious. The sweat drips onto my hand again.

I look at it.

A pool of dark red liquid lay across my knuckles. I look up, unfazed, I'm all alone in a swarm of people, chaos all around me. The fire is blazing in front of me, uncontrollable. I can see what looks like people running around in front of me in orange and yellow clothing, but it all blurs together.

I sit there watching as a figure walks out of a cloud of pitch-black smoke with a body slouched in their arms.

Someone starts screaming, it's a dull scream. That's when I notice the ringing in my ears. For the longest time, I can't pick out what she's saying, what anyone is saying, people are talking all around me, talking to me and it's all blurring together, I can't make out anything.

I'm sorry. Was that something someone was saying? Why?

This was an *accident,* right? What even happened? I shake my head confused. Looking down at my hands I notice that they are shaking uncontrollably and someone else's hands are on top of them trying to calm them. It's not working. I followed these hands up to a face. Green eyes. His lips are moving, I can't make out what he's saying. I look down slightly and the skin under his eyes looks wet. I look down at his hands again and I notice this time that they are a dark red and covered in what looked like blood?

Everything is still blurred. I'm so confused, why am I in pain, why am I sitting here in the grass? Why is my head pounding and why are my ears ringing?

Why?

I look up and I see him smiling at me.

It hits me.

Chapter One

S lap! Her right-hand smashes against my face leaving a mark I know will still be there in the morning. She grabs my ponytail and shoves my face to the ground, my chin hitting the floor first and I cringe slightly, recognizing the feeling that will cause a bruise the next day.

"You little bitch," she spits at me, holding my head to the floor. "I know what you did, you selfish piece of garbage! Stealing from me, when I provide the food you eat and the roof over your head. How dare you take my last cigarette!" She screams the last part louder than the rest. She's angry and drunk.

She gets up from the ground and starts walking in circles wobbling and tripping over her own feet. She's babbling on and on about how she knows there were still cigarettes left in her pack last night. She constantly does this; she gets drunk and finds an excuse to beat the shit out of me. This time, she decided to accuse me of stealing her last cigarette which I watched her pull out of the pack and smoke last night.

Judith, forty-three years old, looks like she's in her fifties. She has smoked and drank herself into old age, her hair is starting to get thin streaks of grey in it. Standing there, slouching, she looks at me and her eyes are bloodshot. She just seems so tired and beat up, it's sad really, she used to be so beautiful. She did it to herself. Her dark brown hair that used to be long and flow so gracefully, is short with obvious split ends from a distance and it is constantly falling out. In fact, I can see a small bald spot on the left side of her head from here.

After a few minutes she notices me staring.

"Stop staring and stand up! Face me like a woman you fucking cow!" She spits at me. I quickly stand and do as she says, knowing this doesn't end well for me. It never does. I only hold on as long as I can to lessen the abuse for Porter, my little brother. She straightens, as much as her broken body can, and starts laughing. I stand there, knowing anything I do or say will only make things worse. So, I stand there, and I wait. I know she has more to say.

"Oh, you're no fun!" she says with a smile on her face and starts staggering closer to me, bottle in hand. "You weren't even wanted, you know," she slurs.

I have heard this one way too many times. I was a mistake. I'm the reason my father is gone. They never wanted me, and the pressure of an unwanted child drove him away. This is one of my favorites. She goes on and on for a while spitting in my face.

"Oh, COME ON!" she yells right in my face. "Say something, you coward!"

I say nothing and stare at the floor expressionless.

"Oh, you are so weak. You will always be weak, just like him!" She yells and then smirks and starts laughing again. Looking down at the bottle in her hand, she looks up at me again and then tightens her grip around its neck. Then in one swift motion brings it up and swings it, hitting me on the right side of my head with the end of the bottle. My head begins to throb, and I start falling backwards.

I fall to the floor and hear a thud as something rolls into my line of sight. The last thing I see before everything goes black, is something I recognize very well. The writing on the bottle, *Dark Valley Porter.*

* * *

When I regain consciousness, she is stumbling to her bedroom and Porter is sitting over me, looking at me with sadness. Some people might mistake this look as pity, except Porter and I don't pity each other.

We feel for each other, sure, yet we will never pity each other. He stands up slowly once she's out of sight and I notice a new bruise on his right arm growing darker as the minutes pass. He grabs a bag of something frozen from the freezer with a kitchen towel and hands it to me. Taking it, I place it where the bottle met my skull and immediately pull it away, flinching.

When I see the towel, I'm not surprised to see blood. It's not uncommon for Porter and I to see our own blood. In fact, it's common. Surprisingly, only one time so far, severe enough for the hospital.

About three years ago, being a stubborn fourteen-year-old, I still had a lot to learn about Judith and how to deal with her.

Porter was getting her a bottle of beer from the fridge, seven years old at the time, slipped on something spilled on the floor from earlier, probably beer, and dropped the bottle completely shattering it. Judith immediately started screaming. She walked over to him and picked up the neck of the bottle, the bottom sharp and broken. I had instantly gotten up, terrified that she might kill him this time.

I ran to them as quickly as possible. When I reached them, she had already raised the bottle in her hand and was on her way to swinging it toward him. Instead, I grabbed her arm and she swung around and looked right at me, her eyes wild with malice.

She ripped her arm from my grip and swung that arm toward me instead. The end of the bottle cut deep into my face. I vividly remember the throbbing pain from the top of my right cheekbone down to the end of my jawline. Blood had begun to pool in my hand as I tried to reach for my face. Surprisingly Judith rushed me to the hospital then and to this day, I don't remember what excuse she gave them as to what had happened to my face.

Porter sat down next to me and brushed my cheek where my scar lay. Somehow, I think he knew that's what I was thinking of. I just smiled slightly and motioned toward the freezer.

"You should get one for yourself, bud. That arm just keeps getting darker." I say. He gets up and grabs a bag of frozen peas from the freezer for himself then walks back over. I get up onto the couch and open my left arm up for him to squeeze in. He lays there, and I wrap my arm around his little body, and he falls asleep.

I kiss him on the forehead softly. "I love you, Porter." I whisper.

I sit there and think, my body not letting me sleep. I think a lot, and I think about a lot.

I think about what could be and I face the facts of what is. It's hard to have hope in this life and yet I do. I have hope for Porter, that maybe enough of my influence can save him from her. I have hope that my plan will work, and I can save us from this hell. I have hope because of Porter, it's selfish to say, but I wouldn't survive this life without him. He is my life.

It's nice sitting there with him, relaxing. I know it won't last though; I am already thinking of all the things I have waiting for me to be done. I have about four hours of sleep before I need to start our day.

Slowly I get up, gently laying Porter down on the couch and move to the chair in the corner. I begin to fall asleep, hoping that I don't dream. It's always either a nightmare or a fairytale, both make it hard to get up the next day.

The alarm clock I shove under the couch cushions to muffle its sound wakes me up, I look around and notice all the little messes I'll be cleaning today. If it weren't for me living in this house, Judith and Porter would be living in filth. She's drunk most of the time anyway. I don't think she'd mind, or even notice.

I walk to the kitchen and glance around at every messy surface. I may as well get the cleaning over with. The kitchen is my least favorite mess to clean because it's right next to where Judith sleeps. Too many times when I was younger, I accidentally dropped something or made some sort of loud noise that woke her up. Waking her up is one of the last things anyone would want to do, especially if she's hungover, which is most of the time.

Bottles upon bottles are scattered across the counter, and some are on the floor. There are too many bottle caps to count and a plentiful amount of spilled liquids on the small 5x6 tile kitchen flooring. Quietly, I grab our plastic trash can, remove the lid, and gently set the bottles in the bottom, placing caps in as well. I throw in all the random trash and put the trash can in the living room. Grabbing a towel and disinfectant spray from the small closet next to the bathroom, I take two simple steps to my left back to the kitchen. The counters, covered in ash and partially dried beer, take little time to clean. The kitchen floor is the same. I clean our trailer every morning, so it's easy to clean from only one day's mess.

Every morning, Porter gets a little sack lunch and Judith gets a steaming half cup of coffee and half cup of liquor. I start the coffee maker and grab a paper bag from a cabinet just to the left of the fridge. Filling it with a basic peanut butter and jelly sandwich, an apple and an empty cheap, plastic water bottle. After pouring the cheap vodka into a mug for Judith I check the bathroom for puke. Unfortunately, this morning I'm unlucky enough to find throw up splattered all along the side of the toilet dripping off the rim and onto the ugly pink tile floor. Cleaning this used to disgust me, and it still does, however at this point I've cleaned puke so many times that I can clean it, start to finish without gagging.

Once the bathroom is all finished, I head for the living room and start trashing all the cigarette butts I can find. I grab all the bottles and caps and toss them in the trash bag. I walk around and double check that there are no mystery puke spots. Scanning the ground my eyes slowly go over the big black burn mark on the carpet in the left corner next to the door.

This is where Judith decided to put out her cigarette on the carpet, unfortunately she didn't put it out all the way and caught the carpet on fire. It wasn't a huge deal because I had stashed a big bucket of water just outside the house for situations just like this. We were lucky the fire hadn't started on one of the many spots where there had been alcohol spilled. We now just had a giant black spot on our carpet floor.

When the kitchen is finished, I grab Porter some clothes from a tub I stash under the couch for the few clothes that we own.

I pull out some bread, quietly spreading on the peanut butter, and fill a glass of water. I walk over to him and gently wake him up, hand him his clothes, and kiss him on the forehead. He heads to the bathroom to change, and I plate the bread for him.

Porter finishes his breakfast and drinks half the glass of water and then glances at me quickly, I give him a look and he finishes it off. I chuckle a little when he hands me the empty glass smiling cheek to cheek, looking very proud of himself. I walk around the counter and give him his backpack, following him as he heads out the door.

We start our walk to the little communal spot where the bus stops for kids who don't live in an area for pick up, which, we don't.

It's about a thirty-minute walk from our trailer. This can be really annoying at times, and it's also a convenient time for me to check in on Porter without there being any chance of Judith showing up.

"So, how are you doing today bud?" I say and look at him with a smile, he looks up at me tired and I notice the stretching of his shirt where he's been pulling it down to cover where Judith made her first mark of the week on him the night before. I stop us and pull his sweatshirt from his backpack and slip it on over his head.

A few years ago, I had to teach Porter different strategies to cover-up the bruises just in case he had to when I wasn't around. Porter obviously still hasn't quite got the hang of it.

When I pull away, we start walking again and I realize I forgot to put on my makeup this morning to cover the bruise just under my left eye. Slowly, I lift the hood of my sweatshirt, pull out my emergency sunglasses from the pocket, and throw them on.

I almost never forget, still for some reason, this morning just feels a little off. Porter notices this and looks away, not making eye contact.

"It's not that bad Stelly, and the glasses cover most of it. Don't worry too much." He says and smiles gently. "And I'm no different than any other morning." He says this very nonchalantly, with little emotion. It hurts knowing that he is so used to this. Sometimes I feel like he feels less than I do, this is all he knows. I grew up with a real mother and a father for the first seven years. This is all he has ever known.

"How is your head?" he asks with obvious concern. I smile at him gently and then tussle his hair.

"Nothing for *you* to worry about, kid. I'm okay." I lie about the pull him into a gentle side hug.. My head was throbbing with every step I took. I think the massive bump that was there last night only grew, nonetheless, I wasn't about to tell him that. He had enough to worry about.

Walking around the corner, I could see the drop off on the right side of the street. We crossed the street and sat down until the bus came. It was only a few minutes before I could smell the strong odor of gasoline the giant yellow school-bus creates. The big yellow giant pulls up to the stop and a herd of kids begin filing through the doors as soon as they open. Porter looks up at me, gives me a big hug and runs off to the bus. I watch as it pulls out, around the corner and soon disappears.

Walking back is often times enjoyable to be alone for a few, yet I would still choose Porter's company over being alone any day.

I love that boy. I kick the gravel under my feet with my torn, dirty, high-top Chuck Taylors. My clothes aren't much better. All my jeans I have had for over three years, and my shirts possibly even longer. I honestly don't remember the last time we were able to buy new clothes. Every once in a while, if our shoes get too worn or a pair of jeans rips I'll have to pull from my savings to replace them, but I try to limit that as much as possible. I need my savings if my plan is going to work. I cross over to the sidewalk and start my thirty-minute walk back to hell.

* * *

When I get to the trailer, I'm relieved to see no signs that Judith has woken up. I quietly open the unlocked door and walk in. Throwing her coffee mug into the microwave, I dread what comes next. I shut the microwave door and head into her room to wake her up for the first time. I walk to her side of the bed and tap her arm.

"Get up" I say and collect as much laundry from her room as I can find. When I head for the other room, I glance at the clock above the oven and notice it's only nine. I'm right on time this morning.

I drop the clothes into the laundry basket in the bathroom and pull it into the living room. Heading back into the kitchen I remember thar I need to throw on some make-up. Once that's done and I'm satisfied with my disguising skills I grab our jar of quarters and throw it into the laundry basket with all our clothes.

Laundry basket in hand, I head out the door and set the basket on the picnic bench right outside our trailer. Quietly I grab my journal I have hidden underneath the trailer and head to the laundry room.

Unfortunately, there are only a few washers and dryers in the laundry room on site, so sometimes it's hard to get laundry done, especially if someone else is already using it and I scheduled my times wrong. This is like guessing when John Mcfarley who lives down the Salmon sites or Sue Jedson down the Eagle sites, are going to be using them. Sometimes when I guess wrong, I wind up waiting for Sue to slowly, but eagerly for her age, switch her clothes to the dryers, then wash more clothes, and then switch those. I just end up helping her and sitting and talking with her about her four cats, Gerold, Jenny, Rodger and MiMi, until she heads back down Eagle to her RV.

The laundry room is right on the other side of the hot tub and pool and so in the summertime when lots of kids roll through here on road trips with their parents, it gets really loud which ruins half the fun of being out here and doing the laundry when I'm not working, it can be very peaceful most of the time.

Today, I was only going to use just enough quarters for three loads which was perfect. I never really need to do more than three loads anyway; Porter and I both have so little clothes. Most of the loads consist of Judith's laundry.

After I put all the loads in the washers, I head over to the leasing office to start my shift. About a year ago when Judith stopped paying the rent suddenly, I came into the leasing office and talked with the manager Sara. I told her that my mom was sick and that she was having a hard time working. Sara is a very sweet lady, probably in her late forties, and she made me a deal that if I made sure that the recreation room was cleaned weekly and I kept up with the pool/hot tub each week she would not charge us for our rent. She was also kind enough to offer me a position in the leasing office.

At first, I told her that I wouldn't be able to do that because I had to take and pick up Porter from School every day. Sara once again made an exception for me and let's me work in the leasing office Mon-Fri from open at ten am to two pm so that I have an hour to finish things up around the house.

Today was the same as any other, I got a few phone calls asking if there were spaces available, what our prices were and if we had any long-term spots available. My answers were always the same. There were always spots open as the park wasn't that great and it was in a pretty rough area. Every once in a while, we'd get people stopping by to ask these questions in person and an occasional resident stopping for mail.

However, Joe Thompson was an exception to this, he stopped in almost daily to collect his mail and if he didn't stop in I brought him his mail if he had any. He was one of my favorite people in this park, a sweet little old man who lived alone with his dog Sadie only a few spaces down from us.

The hours go by quickly today and I find myself packing up my things already. I walk to the mailboxes and check to see if there's any mail, I could bring for Mr. Thompson today.

Seeing that there's none, I walk over to the laundry room and collect all the clothes I had switched to the dryer mid shift earlier. Laundry in hand, I take my time walking back to the trailer, enjoying the fresh air and the rest of my time alone.

Out of nowhere one of the large dogs that lives here runs up to me barking. Startled I drop the basket of clean clothes, almost spilling them all over the dirt and gravel. Puffs of dirt cloud up around the basket, getting some of the clothes slightly dirty, but not enough that I can't just brush it off. Once my initial surprise subsides, I recognize the dog immediately.

"Hi Sadie!" I say to the dog and bend down and pet her as she gives me a giant slobbery kiss on the face. Sadie is a Standard Poodle, and she isn't maintained so she looks like a big, happy, mop. I've hung out with Sadie a couple of times when she found me in the leasing office until Joe comes and finds her.

Joe is a decorated vet, I haven't talked to him in detail, all I know is that he had severe PTSD and Sadie helps a lot with that. "Where's Joe, Sadie?!" I said excitedly, standing up, grabbing my laundry basket and calling Sadie to follow me as I take her back to Joe.

"Well, there you are, girl!" Joe says to Sadie in excitement. "Thank you, Stella, for always bringing her back to me. You are a saint, my dear."

"Oh, it's no problem, Mr. Thompson. I'm happy to do it. It's also an excuse to say hello!" I smile.

"Well, I'm delighted to hear it! It's always a nice surprise to see you. You need to come by and stay for more than five minutes with Sadie and I one of these days! We can make lunch and play cards or something." I felt a ping in my chest because I knew it was unlikely I would ever be able to do that. I nodded and smiled anyway.

"I would love to do that sometime. Well, I hope you have a good day, I need to head home and finish up this laundry. Bye Sadie girl! You take care of him!" I say, wave and start walking away. I walk past a few rows of trailers and RV's until I find my own and walk inside.

I walk to Judith's room to check and see if she's still here even though I know her car was not outside, yet I check anyway and am relieved to see that she is not.

I set the laundry basket down on the couch and pull out mine and Porter's clothes folding them and then bring the rest of the basket into Judith's room, folding and putting them away. Walking out of her room I open the bathroom door and put the laundry basket in there. I walk into the living room and pull out our small tub from underneath the couch and put mine and Porter's folded clothes into the tub and push it back under the sofa.

I check the clock and am excited to see that it's almost time to get Porter. I can't wait to see his smiling face. Porter always makes my day. It's about two thirty, I need to leave here at three. I need to start getting dinner ready. I usually try to make something easy and cheap. Tonight, I'm going with grilled cheese and tomato soup. There's not a whole lot of prepping I need to do for that, so I sit on the couch for thirty minutes before I head out the door to get Porter.

* * *

Dinner wasn't too bad tonight, as in, Judith kept to herself for the most part. At one point she dropped her beer on the ground, luckily the glass didn't break, however I did have to clean it up and get her a new one. Which isn't the worst thing in the world.

There was no yelling tonight, and no new bruises waiting to show up the next morning. There's usually only one explanation for this. She was probably at some guy's house before she came here. That always seems to tame her just a little bit.

When we were done with dinner, Judith took herself outside to have her 'before bed cigarette' obviously having bought herself a new pack today. When she was done with this, she would get a beer from the fridge and take it to bed with her. Within fifteen minutes we would hear an empty beer bottle hit the floor and we would know she had finally gone to sleep.

This is when I usually put Porter to bed. Porter is always so happy, even under our circumstances, he is my saving grace. I'm not sure how he can always stay so joyful and be kind to everyone, and yet he somehow manages to pull it off.

Once I'm done cleaning up after dinner, I pull out the blankets to make Porter's bed. His bed is the couch, so not much, still, it's a soft place for him to rest his head. I watch him as he crawls into the bed, I just made for him.

When he looks up at me, I notice one thing he is missing. I bend down and reach under the couch and pull out his teddy and hand it to him. I look into his kind; innocent eyes and he smiles at me. I sit down on the edge of the couch and tell him a story of a family with two dogs and a cat, both parents and a happy normal little life.

Something he and I will always dream of.

Chapter Two

*H*e was looking down at me with loving eyes. I smiled a huge cheesy smile, grabbed his hand, and kept walking. I can't explain how great it felt to have him pick me up and carry me the rest of the way. The soft prickly feeling of the small snowflakes hitting my face sparked up a beautiful feeling inside me. This one small thing made my heart race and my lips curve into a big grin. I started giggling and he put me back down.

"Are you ready for the best day of your life?" He smiled at me and then set the sled at the top of the hill. He grabbed me and set me on top of it. The feeling of the sled underneath me gave me a rush of exhilaration and I was as happy as I could be. This was one of my favorite things to do with him.

The sled was red with white ropes on the side for handles, the ropes were beginning to fray in the middle where I put my hands because of how many times we had done this. One time we even had to replace them because we ripped them in half. The seat of the sled had growing marks from where I sat that were beginning to feel comfortable to me now.

"Okay, are you ready?" He said and, as usual, without any warning he gave me a light push on the back and down the hill I went.

The wind was streaking through my hair and I was screaming in delight. Even though the snow stung as it hit me in the eyes and the cheeks and every other part of me imaginable, I thought this was one of the best feelings in the world. It was the quick run of adrenaline shooting down my spine as the sled slid down the hill at top speed that gave me the most exhilaration.

I felt free.

"That was soooo fun!" I yelled to him as he raced down the hill right behind me. I reached my hand down touching the snow to slow my speed, but I was going too fast and my skin burned against the hard snow. I lifted my hand up and looked at it, it was red and throbbing. Usually this wouldn't be too much of a problem except that maybe fifteen feet in front of me was a huge tree and it really wouldn't take me that long to reach it and crash into it with all my weight.

"Honey, let go of the sled!" he yelled, and I trusted him with all of me so I let go. My body flew backward, and I was dragging in the snow, it slowed me and yanked me off of the sled right as the sled hit against the tree. My heart was racing, my cheeks were flushed and tears were rolling down my face.

I was terrified.

Nevertheless, once he walked into my view everything brightened and I suddenly felt better, the fear completely washing away.

"Daddy..." I whispered.

* * *

I jolt up waking myself up from what some people would call a good dream. To me, it's a nightmare. I try my hardest to forget him every day, yet sometimes my subconscious mind brings him back. I don't like to remember the good times because eventually I have to remember that he left.

He was my best friend which is why it hurts so much. The fact that he chose to leave me, all alone with Judith. All alone to become a mother myself. The day he left is drilled into my head, that is a day that I will never forget. So much emotion and heartbreak, I didn't just lose my dad, I lost my mom that day too.

I have to force myself to forget it, every once in a while, it still comes flooding back. When it does every detail, every emotion of that night comes flooding back right along with it. Like it was yesterday.

* * *

I was sitting in my room reading my favorite book when I heard a loud crash in the kitchen, I jumped out of bed and ran toward the noise. I was rounding the corner of the hallway to the kitchen when I heard my mom yell.

"I'm not lying to you! You know I would never do something like that! I could never hurt you like that…" I hear her voice trail off as she starts to cry, and I stop in my tracks and watch from the edge of the hallway.

"Why do I not believe you?" My dad says as I watch tears stream down his face. I have never seen him cry before.

Not like this.

"I DON'T KNOW!" My mom screams, throwing another plate in the same spot it looks like she threw the last one. "I have given you no reason to not trust me."

"Oh really? And what about all those late nights you spent at the office with that guy at work, almost exactly twelve months ago?!" My dad yells this time and points his finger at Porter's tiny three-month-old body in the other room.

"Oh my god. Are you serious?" She says, honestly sounding surprised. "You know that was work! And it's not like WE weren't trying!" She yells through her tears.

"I just—" My dad starts to say something and then more tears fall down his cheeks. "I can't do this right now; I need to get out of here." He says and walks over to my mom and kisses her on the forehead with pain spread deeply throughout his face.

I run out from the hallway.

"Daddy no! Where are you going?" my seven-year-old voice yells up at him. I grab his pant leg and he looks down at me with

sad eyes bending down to my eye level.

"Sweetheart, you know how much I love you right?" He says to me, I nod my head as tears stream down my face.

"Well, baby, I have to go away for a little bit, but I will be back for you. I promise, I will come back for you." He strokes my cheek and gives me a sad smile, a tear falling over his lips. "I love you so much." He says and more tears trickle down his face as he stands up and looks at my mom. "Goodbye Judith."

He turns away and walks out the door, car keys in hand. I look over at my mom and she crumbles to the ground.

"Mommy, what's going on?" I look at her terrified. She doesn't say anything, she just motions me over and opens her arms. I snuggle in and she just holds me for hours.

The next morning, is when it all changed.

When I woke up, I walked into the living room and when I didn't see my mom I headed to the kitchen and saw her sitting on the kitchen floor, blank expression, and cigarette in hand. She lifted her hand numbingly slow, breathed in and then filled the kitchen with smoke as her hand flopped back down to her lap. It was almost as if she wasn't there, the only thing proving her presence in the room was the white cloud circling around her. She didn't even notice me standing there watching her. This was the first time I had ever seen her smoke a cigarette and it wouldn't be the last.

* * *

He *lied*.

Ten years ago he lied to me and he left us, left *me* and he didn't come back, didn't fulfill his promise. I can already feel the lingering pain of missing him begin to fill my body. I never let myself feel like this for very long. I don't have time for it and some days if I let it in, it ruins my whole day.

I sit like this for a few more minutes. Finally, I force myself up before I don't have the strength anymore. Looking around the dark room, I realized that I had fallen asleep on the floor with my body leaned up against the couch. I must have fallen asleep mid bedtime story to Porter.

I look at his sleeping face, so relaxed. My chest starts to warm, and my body begins to calm down at the sight of him and a slight smile creeps onto my face. He's my world now, and I'm happy that he is.

It's about four in the morning, which leaves me just a little over an hour before I really need to start my morning. Knowing I won't be able to go back to sleep, I slip on my converse and quietly step out the front door.

I grab my journal from underneath the trailer and sit down on the picnic table out front. When it's quiet like this, it can be so peaceful here. I open the journal and go over the list of things I need to do today that I wrote for myself last night.

- clean
- breakfast

- porter lunch
- porter school
- work
- check out a library book
- groceries

I run my finger over the list, it's basically the same as any other day, except I don't really need to check out a library book. It's code for me to double check my savings that I have stashed in a few different pairs of socks in our clothing tub. I can't have money sitting around somewhere obvious or Judith will see it and use it on cigarettes or alcohol.

The money I have saved is vital to my plan for us to escape. So, for her to find it would be devastating. Soon, soon I'll get us away from here.

At some point today I'll need to go to the grocery store, I usually do this on the weekends, so Porter and I don't have to walk home in the dark.

Unfortunately, we ran out of a few things this morning like bread, which I need for Porters breakfasts and lunches for the rest of the week, and it's only Tuesday. I'm not entirely sure where Judith gets her money to spend on her addictions, but I have started paying for things for Porter and myself.

Part of the reason I got a job in the first place was because Judith rarely ever brought home food and when she did, there was almost never enough for Porter and me both to have one meal a day. Luckily, at that point in time, I was still going to school and Porter and I were able to get meals at school. Once I decided to get a job I knew with everything else I was taking care of at home that I'd need to get my GED, or there was no way I would be able to do it all.

I stay like this for the rest of the hour that I have and watch as the sky slowly becomes brighter. I like to think of the sky as my friend. I can relate to the sky, it goes through so many different stages every day. Every night it gets dark and goes through a state of sadness, and yet every morning it gets bright again, evolving into a new state of hope. I live a life the same as the sky, at some point every day a part of me goes dark, and occasionally, I can see a glimmer of hope, when there are stars in the night sky or no clouds surrounding the morning sunrise.

Thud! Shit, she's up way earlier than usual. I break out of my thoughts, shove my notebook back under the trailer and run inside. I'm surprised to turn the corner that looks to Judith's room and see she's still sleeping. Not knowing where the noise came from I scan the rest of the house and for the first time realize that Porter is half awake rubbing his eyes on the floor where I assume he had just rolled to off of the couch. He looks up at me surprised a little and probably confused by the worried look on my face. My heart rate slows and my hands stop shaking now that I know there's not going to be a confrontation.

Porter sits up and starts to grasp what had happened and realizes why I might have been worried. I sit next to him on the floor and grab his small hand in mine and smile at him before I motion for us to start our morning. It looks like this morning's sunrise will luckily start free of clouds.

Chapter Three

I look at the face staring back at me in the small, cloudy bathroom mirror. Sad, light grey eyes, I look down at my small button nose and heart shaped lips, all surrounded by dark brown almost black hair falling all the way down to my lower back. Reaching my hand up, I run my finger along the ugly scar on the right side of my face, I trace the yellowing bruise on my left cheekbone to the much deeper purple one on my chin where my face had smashed against the floor the other day. Even without the repeating ugly marks on my face, one permanent, I still am not sure that I'd be pretty.

I move on from staring at myself and begin the process of covering as much of the bruising as I can. The yellow one will be easy enough, it's just the purple one that might be a little more difficult, even though I've done this almost every day for about five years. When I first taught myself, I obviously wasn't very good, hence constantly wearing hoods and sunglasses when I could. With all the practice I had, it didn't take me very long to get good enough that I didn't *need* the hood anymore, at this point I just wanted it, it gave me calm.

"Okay bud, you ready to go?" I whisper as I walk out of the bathroom. I look up and he's standing by the front door grinning from ear to ear, backpack, shoes, and jacket on, lunchbox in one hand, peanut butter bread in the other.

"I guess you're ready then" I comment under my breath and walk over to him nudging his side as his dirty blonde hair moves slightly, he looks up at me with his brown eyes. We're both a pretty interesting mix of our parents, I have Judith's dark hair and dad's grey eyes, where Porter has dads blonde hair and Judith's brown eyes. I think the brown eyes are about the only similarity he has to Judith though. From what I can remember, which is not much, he's almost the spitting image of our dad. Except he's not our dad, he's Porter, and he would never leave me.

We walk outside and I look back once at the trailer, imagining ghost like figures of the mom and dad I used to have, I imagine my dad trotting down the steps, keys jingling in hand yelling at us to wait up and get in the car. A small name plate on the lawn in front of the trailer, one that my mom would have decorated just for us. 'The Petersons' what a lovely family we could have been.

"Stelly?" I snap my head back around and look at Porter holding my hand, he smiles up at me effortlessly. "You okay?" He asks. I smile down at him and give him a light nod; squeezing his hand and we start walking.

The walk to the bus stop felt very short today, we're here a little early with no sign of the school bus yet. Porter and I walk over to the bench and sit down together. He starts to tell me about how he really doesn't want to go to his math class today. He tells me that his teacher is a real 'meanie'. I laugh to myself a little. He continues to explain that he feels like she makes the questions too hard and never explains the answers or really takes any time to teach them. He doesn't like her because she grades really hard too, and 'she's always just sitting on her butt reading something at her desk' he whines to me. I laugh a little again.

"Well, if you want I can come in and rough her up a little?" I smirk at him and smack my fist against my palm, twisting it back and forth against my skin. He looks me up and down assumably taking note of my small five foot one figure. He smirks and then starts laughing so hard he bends over and when he looks up again, still laughing I might add, a happy little tear creeps out of his eye.

"What?" I say to him laughing along with him.

"Stelly, I don't think you could beat anyone up if you tried." He lets out one more laugh and then stops and I know we both had the same thought.

33

I can definitely get *beat up though.* We both look down at the ground for a second and then Porter looks up at me and I know he's looking at the spots where my bruises are that I have masterfully disguised.

"Hey" I say to him and smile. "Why don't you do all you can today in your math class and when you get home tonight, I'll see what I can do about helping you with some of that homework." I smirk at him. "You know, your big sis is kind of a genius with math." It wasn't a lie either, it was the only class I always got an A in.

We both look up as we hear the sound of the big yellow bus approaching. "Alright kid, have a good day! I love you." I say and give him a hug pushing his little body toward the bus as it stops.

"I love you too Stelly!" He yells back at me as he runs to the bus and jumps on. I'm about to turn around and start my walk home when I hear another large engine pulling up quickly to the parking area around this bus stop.

The big white and grey Ford truck comes to a screeching halt and a young boy runs out with an older boy in tow. I watch as the older boy pats the younger one on the head as he runs onto the bus behind Porter. The older boy then turns around and is about to walk back to his truck when he turns back and looks directly at me.

I am suddenly very aware that I have been standing here staring at them through this whole process. He stops walking, cocks his head to the right, looking somewhat confused. He seems as if he's about to walk over to me and before I turn away not wanting to talk to anyone, I notice something somewhat familiar about him. Green eyes, bright enough that I could distinguish their color from here. I feel like I've seen them before. Just before he's about to walk over the bus starts up and drives off putting it between the older boy and me. I take this chance to put up my hood and walk off quickly.

Why did he look at me like that? Did he see the bruises? Did he recognize me from somewhere? *Green eyes.* Why did they seem so familiar? I feel like I know those eyes from somewhere, I just can't think of where. I keep walking home, racking my brain as to where I knew this guy from, hoping he didn't notice any marks on my face.

When I get back to the trailer park I head into the office to start my shift. The office is tidy today which means Sara was most likely the last person in here. I sit down at my desk and sitting on top of my tabletop calendar is an envelope with my name written on it in Sara's neat handwriting.

My pay for this week, as usual, is cash. Normally Sara wouldn't pay anyone in cash but she's kind enough to be understanding of my situation and has always made the effort to pay me this way. I open the envelope and count out five hundred and eighty dollars, which is more than twice the amount of my usual week's pay. I put the money back in the envelope, about to call Sara and let her know she made a mistake when I snag my finger on another small sheet of paper in there. I pull it out and it's a note from Sara.

Stella,

Thank you for all your hard work here. I can't put into words how appreciative I am of you. You always leave things so organized when you're done with your shift, and it helps anyone coming in after you. You go above and beyond. Really. I know I'm usually here to hand you your week's pay in person, however I will be out of town for the next couple of weeks, so I left it here for you last night. I knew you would be the next one coming in, so I wasn't too worried about leaving it here. I put in extra for next week's pay as well, as I will still be out of town. I also left you an extra $100 as a thank you for all your hard work. Please just accept the extra pay, you deserve it. I will call you when I have a few extra minutes to give you any more details you might need while I'm gone.

Thanks,

Sara

I fold the note and put it back into the envelope. I don't know if Sara understands how much she just helped us. The extra hundred dollars will go a long way for Porter and me, especially in helping us save up for when I turn eighteen. I put the envelope into my bag and begin setting up the office for the day, turning on the computer and pulling out the planner I keep here. The front door to the office opens and before I have a chance to look up from the computer Sadie comes running around the table to greet me.

"Hi Sadie!" I scratch her head and lean over so she can give me a kiss. Next walks in Joe. "Hi Joe! You guys are here early today, are you here for your mail?" I say to him with a smile.

"Well, Sadie and I decided to go for a walk this morning and I thought we would stop in and say hi on our way back." Joe says and gives me a big grin. "How's your day going today sweetheart?" He sits down in the chair on the other side of my desk.

"It's okay, just a normal day, normal routine." I flash him a tired smile as I continue to pet Sadie. For some reason when I'm with Joe, I feel like I can just be myself without having to worry about being perfect or a good example. Even though I can't completely be myself, I feel like I can be more open with him than most. He's the first friend I've had in a long, long time.

"I bet you're going through a lot right now, huh? Everything going on with your mom and taking care of your brother takes a toll on you. You're so young to have to take the place of a mom, but I understand your circumstance." He says to me and pats my hand from across the table.

Fear rushes through me at his words and I almost jerk my hand back until I remember that I told him the same story

37

that I told Sara. Relaxing a little, I nod at him not knowing what to say. Even though he doesn't really know what's going on, I can pretend he does, and his words mean a lot. I can feel his kindness and how much he cares from across the desk, it hits me like a wave of warmth, and it takes a lot for me to hold back the tears.

He stays with me there for almost an hour keeping me company. We talk a lot about his wife, and I talk about the latest with Porter and tell him how he's doing in school. I even told him about the weird run in with the older boy this morning and how he looked at me.

Joe just laughs and tells me he probably just noticed how beautiful I was. I laughed awkwardly at his comment, it couldn't be that, because I wasn't beautiful.

"Will I see you on Monday then?" Joe asks me as he gets up to leave.

"I'll be here" I tell him with a smile and watch as he grabs his mail, says bye and he and Sadie walk out of the office, leaving only remnants of their warmth behind.

One of the last things I do before I leave for the day is check the hidden compartment I have here in the office. It's safer here than at home. Judith would probably put me in the hospital again if she ever found what I was hiding here.

I walk around the corner to the back of the office where rarely anyone ever goes and bend down in the darkest farthest section. I push one finger down on the edge of the floorboard and the opposite side lifts up leaving a hole in the floor. I reach my hand in and pull out my journal, the stack of photos and a cheap Polaroid camera. The journal I keep in here is the one I use to document the abuse, the stack of photos are pictures of many bruises that have been left on Porter and me over the years and the Polaroid obviously is to take the photos. I chose the Polaroid because it's instant and I don't have to go anywhere to have photos printed.

I count out the photos and make sure they're all there and then take the time to document the latest abuse in the journal and date it. I also pull out the camera and take pictures of the most recent bruises she left on me. I make sure to date the photos as well.

This is all part of my plan, if I can prove that she's an unfit parent, with enough money saved up, I at least have a chance at getting custody of Porter when I turn eighteen. For now, a chance is enough, I will never stop fighting for us.

* * *

When I get home, I double check to make sure Judith is not here, even though her car wasn't in the driveway and the bedroom is empty, I still check about three times to make sure. I can't let her find my savings or it will be gone.

Once I'm positive she's not here, I pull out our tub under the couch. I reach inside and pull out the three different pairs of socks that hold my savings and turn them all inside out.

The cash falls out onto the floor splaying in a weird awkward pattern. I count about one thousand four hundred and fifty dollars not including what I got today, which means I have about two thousand and thirty all together right now.

I separate out two hundred for this week and put it in my pocket for now putting the rest back into the bag and into the compartment.

I have slowly been adding to my savings over time, using as little as I can over the week to keep building it, so when the time comes, I can prove that I'm stable, that I know how to build a savings and that I have some money to take care of us. It's taken me a little over a year and lots of extra hours to be able to save as much as I have now. I try to put at least a hundred into the savings each month. Sometimes if we're cheap enough for one month or I put in extra hours helping around the park I can put in a little more.

Luckily though, with making sure the recreation room and pool is always tidy on the weekends, I don't have to worry about the monthly rent as well.

When everything is all put away I sit down on the couch and look around the room making sure there's nothing else that needs to be picked up or tidied.

I check the clock and notice I still have about forty five minutes until I have to leave to get Porter. Laying down on the couch I set my small alarm clock for forty minutes from now and decide to take a nap. I close my eyes and can't help but think of the older boy, and those familiar green eyes.

* * *

I'm sitting crisscrossed in the woods, familiar woods. I look down at my body, a six year old body. I noticed a small object rolling toward my leg. It was a very used, dirty old baseball. I pick it up and it feels familiar in my hand, like I've held it a million times before. I look around at where it might have come from and see nothing except trees and a light mist rolling in.

I stand up and start walking, baseball in hand. The mist rapidly begins thickening around me and out of fear I begin running and running and running. Tears start rolling down my cheeks, there's a lingering feeling that this forest used to be filled with such happiness yet this mist filling the air feels dark and wrong.

I trip on a branch and stumble to the ground. Breathing heavy, I pick myself up and look around again. I look behind me and all around me and see nothing, but I feel the weight of the mist coming down on me. Terrified, I start to move my feet again when I hear the rustling of leaves in front of me.

I look up and peeking out from behind a tree is a young boy, only a few years older than me. My body starts to fill with warmth, even with the haze surrounding me. He walks out from behind the tree and waves me to follow him and starts running ahead. Quickly I begin to move my feet and chase after him, stumbling a few times. I keep up with his pace as not to lose him. He makes a few turns and then we're running on a path lined with tall trees swaying in the wind.

As we run, the fog begins to clear and about twenty feet in front of us is a clearing where the sun is shining so bright it almost hurts to look at. The boy runs into the clearing, and I lose sight of him with the sun shining in the background. I finally break through the tree line and into the clearing, the intense feeling of the mist is gone, and I can only feel the warmth of the sun on my skin now. I blink my eyes a few times, and when they finally adjust, standing in front of me is the boy. Bright green eyes look down at me. He's holding his hands out as if he wants me to give him something and I look down at mine, still clutching the familiar baseball. I toss it to him, and he catches it and smiles. He looks down at the baseball in his hand and then back up at me and smiles again. He opens his mouth to say something and then looks down at his hands again.

"Stella, what's my name?"

* * *

"Kaleb!"

I shout and sit upright, waking myself up from my dream. I rub my eyes and think about what just happened and the dream I just had.

My mind is still foggy, but I know who the older boy is and why I recognized him. It was Kaleb, my childhood friend that I used to play with before my life went to shit. His dad and my dad were best friends. How could I ever forget him, or not recognize him instantly? Yet more importantly, why is he here? His family moved away years ago.

Beep beep beep... Looks like I woke up only seconds before the alarm I set. I put on my shoes and head out the door. I have about thirty minutes until I get to the bus stop to pull myself together.

Would I approach him? Do I just ignore him? Will he even be there? It's not like I can have any real kind of friendship with him, the way my life is now. I just need to make sure he doesn't see me again. I can't risk him seeing any marks on me, I can't risk him finding out. Either way I'm not the girl I used to be, so I doubt he'd want anything to do with me. He was friends with the wild, carefree, adventurous Stella. I no longer have time for adventures.

Kaleb and I used to have so much fun together, our dads being best friends, meant we spent A LOT of time together. He was only three years older than me, so we were close enough in age that we got along really well together. Any time one of them would go to the others house, they brought me or Kaleb along.

He was one of the only friends I had and definitely the best one. Our families would get together every Sunday and we'd have barbecues, sometimes game nights or even just dinner together and enjoy each family's company. Our dads weren't the only ones that were close, I remember our moms were actually good friends as well.

There's one Sunday specifically though that I'll never forget. It was our last game night and one of the last times that I saw Kaleb.

It was a normal Sunday for us, and it was a game night. One of our favorite games to play as a group was charades. Our parents always laughed and had smiles on their faces and so did we. This Sunday night we had decided on charades once again. There was an even number of girls and boys, so often we would play girls against boys, but tonight we played my family against Kaleb's.

Kaleb's mom, Cora was her name, was actually really good at charades so having her switch from mine and my mom's team was a difficult thing for us, as the girls almost always won because of Cora.

We had played lots of rounds that night, smiling and laughing, truly just having a great time. We were at my family's house so my mom had made dinner for us. I can still remember the smell of the pot roast slowly cooking on the counter that whole day. When we had finished eating that night, the adults went off to hang out amongst themselves and Kaleb and I retreated to the back yard. We would talk and throw the dirty old baseball back and forth all night.

This night was different though, I had tossed the baseball to him again for the millionth time that night and when he caught it, his shoulders dropped and his face fell. I had instantly known something was wrong, so I rushed over to him. He fell to the wet grass as soon as I asked him if everything was okay and so I sat down next to him. He began to tell me that lately his mom had started acting weird, losing energy and that he was really worried about her.

I had grabbed his hand and when he looked up at me, one small tear had fallen from his eye, down his cheek and landed on my hand. I vividly remember exactly where we were sitting in the grass like it was yesterday. I was sitting facing the sliding screen door to the house and Kaleb was facing the woods that we played in growing up. I had a clear view of our parents from where we were sitting.

As Kaleb continued to tell me what he was worried about, I watched the beginning of the end for Kaleb and I unfold right before us. Cora had just gotten up to refill her half empty wine glass. I watched in horror from the cold damp grass underneath me as her wine glass slowly slipped from her hands and her body fell to the floor. I screamed, alerting Kaleb to the situation and we both rushed into the house to check what was going on.

Cora had been laying on the ground before us, her wine glass shattered on the floor next to her with the red liquid spilling all around.

Paul, Kaleb's dad, was sitting next to her crying and yelling for his wife, my mom was sitting next to him crying and shaking her head and my dad was on the phone calling for an ambulance.

I was terrified, and I still sat there. I realized that Kaleb must be feeling even worse, and when I looked over at him, he was just sitting on the floor about two feet from his mom. He was frozen in place; his expression was blank and his entire body was shaking.

I crawled over to him and grabbed his body and held him against me all night. I held him when the ambulance arrived, I held him when they took her to the hospital, and I held him as his dad was telling him he loved him and that he would come back for him tomorrow.

And he let me, he had laid against me, frozen for hours. After a few hours his shaking subsided. Right before my parents separated us and gently put us to bed, I remember the cold feeling of one single tear falling onto my arm.

The next couple weeks were very strange. We hadn't gotten together for a Sunday, and I hadn't seen Kaleb for almost a month. I remember very clearly the phone call I knew would change everything.

My dad had been sitting on the couch and I was sitting next to him. His phone rang and he looked at it for a few seconds before picking it up and answering. Looking back, he had probably known what Paul was going to say. My dad's phone was loud enough that I could hear both sides of the phone call clearly.

Paul says, 'She's dead John, she's gone…' I couldn't hear the next part, but I once again heard very clearly when he said that he couldn't stay here any longer and that he and Kaleb were moving away, that he couldn't just live in the town he had built a happy life. My dad tried his best to console him, to try and convince him to stay, that us and our family would be here for him and Kaleb, that Kaleb needed a friend like me, even so, there was no convincing him, he had already decided.

A week later Kaleb and Paul stopped by the house to say goodbye, but Paul couldn't bring himself to come inside. My dad, mom and I had walked outside to say goodbye, I was sad and even so, I still wanted to say goodbye to Kaleb. When we walked outside it was only Paul standing there. He kept apologizing saying he tried to convince Kaleb to come out and say his goodbyes, but that he didn't want to push him too much. I had watched from behind my mom's body as my dad walked over to Paul and gave him one of his famous bear hugs. I had then looked past them into their car and noticed Kaleb sitting in the car, unmoving with his head down. His face was once again expressionless, yet I still noticed, even from far away, a tint of sadness.

His dad then got into the car, gave us a wave and I watched as Paul drove him and my best friend away. That was the last time I saw Kaleb, until this morning.

Chapter Four

"Stelly... Stella..." I open my eyes and Porter is leaning over me gently shaking my shoulder. "Stelly it's 7:30." He says to me, and I jump up from the chair.

"Shit." I say and start looking around me. I can't believe I didn't set an alarm last night. We're gonna be late if I don't hurry. I run to the bathroom as quietly as I can to change and then throw on some makeup, making sure to cover everything.

I do a quick clean in the kitchen and prep some bread and peanut butter for Porter, putting together a quick lunch for him at the same time.

Fuck Judith, she'll have to make her own coffee this morning. I grab Porter's lunch and tell him to go change. When he's ready, I set down the lunch, hand him his breakfast and throw on my shoes, sloppily lacing them.

It's about eight fifteen so we're basically jogging this morning. "I'm sorry kid, this is my fault today." I say to Porter and tug him along.

"It's okay Stelly, it'll be fine. Maybe I'll even get to skip school today and spend time with you in the office." He is only half joking, so I give him a look and nudge him as we continue jogging to the bus stop. As we turn the last corner to get to the bus stop, the school bus is already pulling away. I drop Porter's hand and start running after it, yelling for it to stop, but we're still too far away and it's gone before I even make it to the waiting area.

"Shit." I say under my breath and turn to walk back toward Porter. He's standing right where I left him smiling brightly. I give him a look. "You're not missing school." I tell him sternly.

"But—"

"No buts, we're walking." He looks up at me shocked as I begin to drag him along.

"Stellyyy, last time it took us like two hours" Porter whines to me.

"That's okay, you'll still have a little over four hours of school left. It's worth it." I grab his hand a little looser than I had been holding it before and pull him next to me so we're standing side by side. It looks like we'll both be getting in a little exercise today and worst case, I'll carry Porter the last half of the walk if I need to. He's not missing school.

We've only made it about a half mile past the bus stop and I can tell Porter is already getting tired. I stop him and motion for him to hand me his lunch and his backpack. He looks up at me and I can tell he's grateful. We start walking again approaching our first turn on the route to the school. I open my mouth to say something to Porter and—

"Stella?"

I whip my body around and stare at him. Kaleb. I recognize him this time, and this time he's only about six feet away from me.

His hair is the same, as blonde as ever, the same as his moms, and his eyes are almost brighter than before. A green I was always drawn to. However, there are some notable differences as well, he looks to be over six feet tall now, and he's not a scrawny little kid anymore. I'm startled at the difference, and not surprised at all, it's been a little over ten years since the last time I saw him. Even so, this twenty-year-old Kaleb, somehow feels just as familiar as the nine year old Kaleb.

"Stell, it really is you." He smiles at me, a warm, welcoming smile I haven't seen in a long time. He begins mumbling to himself almost, about how he thought it was me the other day, but that I was gone before he could say anything. Looking up again, smiling still he starts to take a step and reach out toward me. Instinctively I take a step back

51

and his smile and hand fall at the same time. He just looks at me obviously hurt.

What do I do? I hadn't planned for this. I wasn't going to talk to him. I had already decided I wasn't going to see him again; I was going to make sure he didn't see me. I was in such a rush this morning I didn't even think about it, and I didn't prepare. I sigh to myself and look up at him.

"What are you doing here?" I say to him almost in a snarl. "You moved away a long time ago. Why did you come back?" I say to him and look down at my feet.

"Who's this here?" Kaleb says completely ignoring my questions, smiling again just instead of at me, he's smiling at Porter. He starts to walk over and then bends down to eye level with him. I look down at his little self, he's surprised, and he's got a big ass grin growing on his face.

"I'm Porter!" He explains, then motioning to me. "The grumpy one is my older sister." He says and they both begin laughing at his remark. "Who're you?" Porter says excitedly pointing directly between Kalebs eyes. Cross eyed looking at Porter's finger, Kaleb laughs and then grabs Porter's tiny hand in his large one and begins to shake it.

"It's nice to meet you Porter, I'm Kaleb." He said this so brightly and some part of my icy center began to melt a little bit. I knew better. Knowing Kaleb again was dangerous. I just couldn't risk it.

"Well, it was good seeing you, but we'll be going now." I say to Kaleb and begin to turn away when Kaleb grabs my shoulder, turns me toward him and pulls me to his chest. He wraps his heavy arms around me and for a second, I let him because something about these arms felt so familiar.

"I've missed you." Kaleb says quietly against my ear. I almost fell into him and let his arms swallow me in warmth, but then I feel Porter's tiny hand still wrapped in mine and it brings me back to my senses.

I push Kaleb away and just look at him. He's still smiling at me, and there's a flicker of disappointment in his eyes that wasn't there before. It doesn't matter, I can't have a friendship with him anymore. It's just not possible. It's better he be disappointed now.

"I'm sorry Kaleb, we really need to go. I've got to get him to school." I hear my voice naturally softening toward him.

What am I *doing*?

I have to make it clear to him that there's no future friendship for us. My life is different now, more complicated. I won't let my feelings or my desires for a friend get in the way of my life with Porter, and it's way too possible that recreating a friendship with someone from my past life could do just that.

It could destroy everything.

"...you do!?" I focus back in at the sound of Porter's voice. Apparently they've been carrying on a conversation while I was lost in thought.

"Wait, wait." I say and look at them both. "You do, what?" I say and look at Kaleb.

"I have a truck." He says and smiles at me mischievously. "And I'm gonna use it to take you guys to school." He smiles at me again. No, no, no, no.

"No." I say and look down at Porter's shocked face. "We're fine walking." At that I grabbed Porter's hand, tired of this, and pulled him along.

"But Stelly, I thought you guys were friends. I don't want to walk another two hours to school, I'll basically miss the whole day." I look down at his pleading face. "Pleeeaaaaassse." He whines up at me and I sigh, knowing I can't say no to him.

"Fine. Just this once. It's back to the bus after school today and moving forward." Porter ignores the second part of what I said and begins jumping up and down in excitement and then runs over and gives Kaleb a big hug. Kaleb looks shocked at first and then his expression softens into a smile, as he hugs him back. Porter grabs Kaleb's hand and they begin walking toward his truck parked only a few blocks away. I watch as the two boys walk in front of me and can't help it, I feel like a third wheel.

I roll my eyes and follow after them.

* * *

The whole ride to the school, Porter was talking Kaleb's ear off, and Kaleb seemed to love it, smiling and laughing the whole time.

I just sat on the other side of Porter with my arms crossed, I couldn't help but feel a little jealous. It was honestly shocking how fast Porter warmed up to Kaleb, usually it takes longer for Porter to get comfortable around new people. The only other person Porter talked to like this was me, and for some reason Porter seemed to take a liking to Kaleb.

"So, what were you doing at the bus stop the other day?" I ask Kaleb without looking at him.

"She speaks!" Kaleb says and I roll my eyes, feeling his gaze on me. He chuckles and then continues to explain. "I moved back out here about six months ago actually. I stayed with my uncle for the first two and then I got my own place. My cousin is about Porter's age and my uncle had some thing's going on this week, so he asked me to take him to the bus stop. I insisted that I could take him all the way to school, but apparently my cousin really likes riding the bus with his friends."

It was silent for a few minutes after that. I wasn't good at this conversation thing. The only people I really talked to were Joe and Porter.

"That's nice of you." I say breaking the awkward silence.

"What's your cousins name?" Porter asks. He's sitting in the middle seat between Kaleb and me. He seems to love this,

I'm not sure if it's just because we're going somewhere in a car instead of walking or taking a bus, or if it's because he feels like he's making a new friend.

"James, do you know him?" Kaleb asks, directing the conversation back to Porter.

"Yeah, he's in my class. He's super nice and everyone at school loves him." Porter says with a small smile. "I talk to him sometimes; I just don't really have a whole lot of friends. Most of the kids in my class like to hang out outside of school a lot and I can't really hang out outside of school." My eyes go wide at this, and I nudge Porter's side slightly. "Oh." He says embarrassed and quickly says after. "It's okay though, because I have Stelly, and we hang out a lot." I was hoping Kaleb missed it and would just move on from the subject, unfortunately he didn't.

"Why can't you hang out outside of—" I interrupt before he can say anything else.

"Our mom's sick, so we can't have people over. And she doesn't like Porter going to people's houses she doesn't know, and she's not in a place to meet people right now." I said, telling him the same lie I tell everyone else.

I look at Kaleb's face and it has almost an unnoticeable sadness to it that I feel like I've seen before. He looks like he wants to say something, but we're pulling up to the school now, so he doesn't press the issue.

Once we pull up to the front doors, I jump out of the truck and grab Porter's backpack and lunch for him. I help Porter out of the truck and shut the truck door, give him a hug and send him on his way.

Kaleb waves goodbye too and Porter waves back. Once I see that Porter is inside I check the time and it's only eight forty five, which means we beat the bus here. If I leave now then I'll get to the office around eleven, an hour late. That's not great, but if I explain the situation to Sara, I'm sure she will understand.

I look up determined to walk home and not take a ride from Kaleb. Rides from him needed to end here, I didn't want him to get the wrong idea just because we accepted one ride from him. I start walking and then smash into Kaleb as he rounds the corner of the truck. Stumbling back, I look up at him and he looks surprised.

"What are you doing?" He asks laughing.

"I'm going home, what else?" I said to him a little more harshly than I had intended. It doesn't really matter though if I'm nice at this point.

"You're going to walk the six miles or even farther, I don't know where your house is, but it doesn't matter. Stel that's crazy, just let me give you a ride, I'll leave you alone after that if that's what you want."

He looks at me with sad eyes, I don't care, I can't budge on this. I roll my eyes, I don't know why he keeps calling me

Stel, it's a nickname from a long time ago. He doesn't know me anymore. He wasn't around to see what my family turned into.

"Why do you keep calling me that? And why do you even care?" I say and look down at my feet.

"What do you mean? I've always called you that." When he says this, he sounds a little sad and I look up at him.

"It's a nickname from a long time ago Kaleb. I'm not the same girl I was back then." When I say this the anger slowly subsides and turns to sadness. I want so badly to just pretend it didn't matter, to let this kind person take me home. But it does.

"I know that, it's obvious just looking at you." He says looking me up and down. "I'm not the same either, a lot has happened since back then, and I'd really love to get to know you again if you'd let me, I couldn't believe my eyes when I saw you the other day—" He cuts himself off and turns away.

"I— I just can't Kaleb." As I say this it seems like something snaps in him, like he just broke out of a daze of sadness and then chuckles to himself.

"Okay enough of this, it's one ride and you'll just have to suffer through my company." Kaleb says and before I knew what was happening, he had picked me up like I was nothing and threw me over his shoulder.

"Wha—" I tried to protest but it was too late, he had already opened the truck, sat me inside it and shut the door.

He climbed into the truck from the driver's side and looked at me. I was glaring at him.

"What the fuck Kaleb." Was all I could think of to say. If I got out of the truck and tried to walk home again, he would just run after me and do the same thing again. He shrugs his shoulders.

"Well, I can say the one thing that hasn't changed about you, is that you are stubborn as hell." He laughs like this is a joke. "Only I'm quite a bit bigger than I used to be, so you can't bully me anymore Stel, things are different now." He says sarcastically then puts on his seat belt and begins to drive away.

"What— I, I never bullied you." I say and look away blushing. "Your ideas were just stupid." And at that a familiar smile crept up on my face and we were both laughing. It felt so good to laugh again.

If being with him was such a risk, why did it feel so good? Why did his presence calm me in such a way, in a way that I haven't felt in so long. It was almost like sitting with Joe, but *different.* It was hard to say no to him if I'm being completely honest. I looked over at him, and he was focused on the road in front of us. It was silent for a while after that.

"Let me take you to get Porter from school today." He says pushing the issue again. "It can be the last time, at least let me do this one thing for you, it really doesn't affect my day that much, I'm happy to do it. If you're worried that it would be asking too much or something—"

"Fine." I say, cutting him off, not completely convinced that it was fine, but it was just one more ride. It would save me time tonight, which I could use. I'll just have him pick me up at a random house in the neighborhood around the corner from the trailer park. It'll be fine, just one more ride. I can't lie to myself though; I've missed him too.

He was a part of a happy life of the past. I had shut out thoughts of him a long time ago, it was one of those things that was just too painful to remember. But, seeing him again, I didn't realize how much I had missed him.

"Really?" He looks at me then, shock written all over his face. "I thought I'd have to do a lot more convincing than that." He laughs to himself. "Well, okay then, do you want me to just come pick you up today to go get Porter after school?" He says and looks at me again, studying my face. I still wasn't sure about this, yet I was excited to have a little extra time tonight.

It was a Friday which means I'd have to help prepare Judith, the house and Porter for her new fling to come by in the morning to get her. She leaves every weekend with a new dude. It usually is someone new, however sometimes she does stick to one for a month or so.

"That's fine. Just know that this is it, Porter and I will go back to our normal routine on Monday." When I say this to him, he laughs again and puts a hand in the air as if surrendering.

"Yes ma'am." He says and I scowl at him. "By the way, where are we going?" I look up surprised that we're already back at the bus stop.

"Oh right." I laugh and look away embarrassed. I give him directions to the neighborhood around the corner from the trailer park and have him park in front of one of the houses. "This is it" I say and point to a small blue house with white trim. I begin to get out of the truck when he grabs my shoulder.

"Wait. In case you need it." He says and hands me a small piece of paper. "Pick you up here at two forty five?" I nod and continue stepping out of the truck, paper in hand.

Once he drives away, I unfold the small paper and see what I assume to be his phone number. I fold it back up and put it into my jeans pocket.

* * *

With Kaleb giving me a ride this morning I was able to get home about five past nine, so I had just enough time to get the house cleaned up and head to work. Although the day went by pretty quickly, I couldn't help but notice that my mind had been distracted all day.

My thoughts drifted to Kaleb. I agreed to one more ride. For any normal person this wouldn't seem like such a big deal, however it came with a lot of risk for us. Logically speaking, it wasn't a big deal, and it would give me just a little extra time tonight, and I honestly don't think that's the reason I agreed to it. All day I kept trying to convince myself that *was* the reason, yet at the end of the day, I know it's not.

The feeling of talking with someone my own age, of laughing like that again, even briefly, I couldn't ignore it. It was almost as if some of the cold, dark black coal inside me found a spark again. One I had forgotten about.

When I'm with Porter it obviously brings me happiness, I love him, he is what I live for. I would give my life for him. And it's a different kind of happiness, one that comes with responsibility. Porter is my little brother, I must protect him, provide what I can for him. At seventeen, that can sometimes feel like an unbearable weight I can't shake off.

And, for some reason, even if it was just a few minutes, being alone with Kaleb almost felt like part of that weight was chipping away. I felt a freedom I almost can't remember feeling before. I didn't need to protect this man, I felt like I could just be me, with no extra responsibility. And then I walked back into the house this morning and the little weight that I thought chipped away piled right back on.

I was being selfish. Even though he seemed to be good for Porter too, I was thinking selfishly. As good as it felt having him around, I need to remember to keep him at a distance. If Judith found out that we were even just taking a ride from someone else, she would lose it. Not only that, but if Kaleb found out about Judith, I'm terrified he would say something.

This could get really messy if I'm not careful. For Porter's sake, I have to keep my distance. This needs to be the last ride, the last time I see him.

I got to the little blue house Kaleb had dropped me at earlier about two thirty-five. Ten minutes before our agreed pick up time in case Kaleb arrived early, I didn't want him to see me walking to the house. I sit down on the curb out front so as not to draw too much attention to myself, standing in front of some random person's house.

Looking down at my worn converse I hear the familiar sound of the large engine coming around the corner. I look up and there's Kaleb smiling brightly as he pulls up next to me, puts the grey and white truck in park and waits for me to hop in. I open the heavy door and pull myself inside.

"Hey." I can hear the smile in his voice as he says this. I turn my head to look at him and sure enough, his ear-to-ear grin shines brightly toward me.

"Hi." A half smile pulls on my cheek as I buckle my seat belt. I just need to remind myself that he's not my friend, he's just giving me a ride today. That's it.

"How was your day?" Kaleb asks this as he begins to drive off towards Porter's school.

"It was good, just a normal work day, how about you?" I shift in my seat, slightly uncomfortable and not knowing what else to say.

"It was pretty good, just work." He says and continues to focus on the road.

Most of our ride was quiet, I'm really not great at conversation. I overthink it and end up just not talking unless something needs to be said. Kaleb doesn't really seem like the type that wouldn't be good at conversation though. I'm not entirely sure if he's staying quiet because I make him uncomfortable or if he's just trying to be respectful of me in some weird way. Either way as soon as we pick up Porter, the cab of this truck will be bouncing around with noise.

"Thank you." I say and look at Kaleb and then down at my hands. He looked almost surprised when I said this. Even though I probably won't see him again after today, I want to make sure he knows that I appreciate the time he took out for us. Today was the last day he would be picking up and dropping off his cousin at the bus stop, so after today there won't be any reason to see him. Kaleb will once again become just a part of my past.

"You're welcome."

I'm not sure what else to say to him so I'm just willing the time to go by and for us to get to the school faster. Sure, enough we turn a corner and are pulling up to the front of the school.

Porter is standing out front waiting for the bus it looks like. I guess I did tell him this morning that we wouldn't be riding with Kaleb again so I shouldn't be surprised. But Porter was. A smile grew on his face as he recognized the truck pulling up to the curb.

Even though it was just one day, it seems that having someone else around brought another side of happiness, not just out of me, out of Porter too. I'm hoping that both of us can hold onto this feeling for a little bit longer.

Chapter Five

"STELLA!" I jolt up out of the chair at the sound of her voice.

My mind is still trying to focus on what is going on in the dark living room.

"You piece of shit, did you just completely forget that I was leaving tonight? You didn't even consider that I might want you to be awake when I left? How selfish can you get?!" Judith continues to yell as I fully start to grasp the situation. It's Friday night and Judith is about to leave for the weekend. I check the clock and it's a few minutes after midnight. Only a few hours ago I put Porter to sleep on the couch and began prepping for her to leave. I pulled out all the alcohol I thought she'd want to bring with her and even put a fresh pack of cigarettes on the counter next to the bottles. I made sure the house was clean and that there was nothing of mine or Porter's out in the open or in her way. I'm not entirely sure what she's so upset about this time, I'm never sure so I get up out of the chair and look to see if Porter is still on the couch. I walk over to check on him and he's pretending to sleep, which is obvious to me, yet Judith would never notice.

"I'm sorry for being so inconsiderate, is there something I can do to help before you leave?" I'm trying my best to sound calm and sincere. And of course that's not how she took it. My eyes are starting to adjust to the dark room, and I can see her standing in the kitchen fumbling with the bottles on the counter.

"Was that sarcasm?" She sneers at me, directing a glare that could kill in my direction.

"No ma'am, I was just trying to help." She scoffs and motions to the bottles on the counter. I walk over and reach to grab the bottles when she grabs my arm before I can grab them.

"Don't fucking try to be cute. Lose the fucking attitude." She pulls the finished cigarette out of her mouth and puts it out on my sleeve. I hold my breath trying not to react to the pain as she shoves it deeper into my arm. Luckily I'm wearing a long sleeve shirt so it doesn't hit my skin directly this time, however it still burns through the shirt and the remnants of embers hit my skin. My arm drops to my side as she lets go and walks past me.

"Bring out the bottles, leave the attitude." She says this and walks out the front door. I hear laughter after about thirty seconds. Grabbing the bottles I walked toward the door. Porter is sitting up slightly on the couch looking at me, asking with his eyes if I'm okay. I nod and motion for him to lay back down.

When I get outside, Judith is standing in front of a guy I don't recognize, so obviously he's new.

Judith turns around and tells me to put the bottles in the back seat of his car. I do and start walking back to the house when she tells me to wait. She walks over to me, and I glance over once at this new guy. He's leaning up against his car, cigarette in hand. He's probably in his early forties, chin length greasy hair and a disgusting look on his face as he looks me up and down. A smirk grows on his face as Judith walks up to me.

"Alright take care of the house for me while I'm gone." Judith gives me a fake smile. She is pretending to be a doting parent now that there's someone else here. She pinches my cheek, let's go and gently smacks my face.

"I'll be back Monday" Judith and this new guy get in his car and drive off. As they're driving out of the park I can faintly see Judith throwing her finished cigarette out the window of the car and then the car is gone.

I walk back into the house and Porter is sitting up on the couch. He walks over to me and gives me a big hug.

"She's gone now Stelly, you can relax." He says this and hugs me tighter. My body automatically begins to slow down. I didn't even realize until it stopped, but my body had been shaking.

I kiss Porter on the head and pull away walking to the kitchen. My arm unfortunately needed to be tended to. Lifting the sleeve of my shirt I see a bright pink circle on my upper forearm. I run it under cold water for about a minute and then wrap it in a clean bandage.

"It wasn't that bad this time, she was only slightly angry." Porter says this as he sits back down on the couch. I nod as I lock the front door before sitting back down in the chair.

"Yeah bud, it wasn't that bad this time." I smile at him, and he smiles back. "We'll make sure to make the most of this weekend while she's gone. How about some games tomorrow?" I say to him and when he doesn't respond I look over to see that he has already fallen back to sleep. I lay back in the chair and drift into sleep myself.

* * *

I wake up to the sun shining through the window into my eyes. Porter is still sleeping so I get up and make myself some coffee. The weekends are easily my favorite part of the week. Even though, part of the day on Saturday I usually spend cleaning up the recreation area of the park, it's still better than the rest of the week. These two days, Porter and I get to be alone, we get to relax just a little bit.

Coffee in hand, I start getting ready while waiting for Porter to wake up. I usually get up around seven on the weekends and Porter usually wakes up around eight or eight-thirty. The house is mostly quiet with the occasional voices drifting through from outside. Looking at my face in the bathroom mirror I notice that the bruising has mostly faded to a light yellow and will probably be gone by tomorrow. I throw on some make-up anyway just to be safe and then pull up my sleeve to change the bandage on my arm.

The small red circle is slightly swollen with small singe marks on the edges but otherwise doesn't look infected. I run my arm under cold water again to relieve some of the pain and then wrap it loosely in a new bandage.

It's not like I'm used to the pain exactly, it's almost like it's just become a part of my body at this point. At some point the pain became a reminder to me that I'm still alive, that my heart is still beating and that this isn't just a horrible nightmare that I'll eventually wake up from. The thought that my body requires pain at this point to remember that it's alive is terrifying. Sometimes it makes me feel hopeless, yet even if I have to suffer with pain for the rest of my life, I don't want Porter to have a life like that.

I take my coffee and walk outside sitting down on the bench. I look around the trailer park at all the people walking around. Some walking around alone and some with their families. I like to people watch because I can imagine what their lives might be like.

I'll sometimes make up stories in my head of who they are and what their life looks like. Like this family that's currently sitting at the park.

There are two kids, they look like siblings and they have both their parents with them. They're either here on vacation or they just moved here because they are new faces to me. The dad is tall, his face is unshaved and he's wearing khaki shorts, a worn t-shirt and some sandals. The mom is also tall and she's in jean shorts that come to just above her knees, a tank top and some sneakers. The kids both look like they've been playing all day, their clothes dirty and unkept. This family is obviously of lower income, the mom's name in my head is Janette and the dad's is Tom.

Tom works a regular office job where he makes enough to keep up with the simple lifestyle they want, while Janette stays home with the kids and occasionally goes to a weekly book club with her friends.

Even though they aren't ridiculously rich or anything Tom and Janette are completely and utterly in love. As long as they have each other and they show their kids what love truly looks like, they're happy with that.

Their family lives a fairly steady lifestyle, so coming here to this trailer park is a good change for them, they needed to get away for a while and do something new.

I like to imagine things like this, play these little movies or write these little stories in my head, it's a great distraction. To look at and evaluate someone else's life even though my evaluation could be completely false. Sometimes when I do this though, my mind will shift to my own family, my own father. Even though I try and keep thoughts of him out, I can't help myself from wondering where he is, or why he left.

I only really know what Judith has told me, and it's not much and none of her stories ever match up or make sense. Every time I've asked, she either didn't respond or got angry and I ended up with a new bruise.

According to Judith, my father left because of many reasons including, he didn't want me or Porter anymore, he left because they never wanted me, and it stressed him to the point of leaving or because he found a new family that he wanted more and left with no trace. I've tried in the past to look through Judith's things but I was always so terrified that she would find out that my searching was very rushed and far from thorough, so I never found anything relating to my dad. I may never know what happened to him, and I'm not entirely sure that I care.

The sound of the door opening behind me makes me jump and I spill some of my coffee onto my hands. Relaxing a little, I have to remind myself that today is Saturday and Judith is not here.

I turn around and see a still sleepy Porter rubbing his eyes. The door is halfway open, and Porter is looking at me as he yawns. I smile at him, and he gives me a tired smile back.

"You're up earlier than usual." I say to him as he walks outside and sits next to me on the bench.

"I heard the door open." Porter looks at me and smiles. "I'm happy about it, cause it means we get to spend more of the day together." He smiles as he lets out another big yawn. I lean over and nudge him slightly, pulling him to my side for a hug.

"Well if you're ready for the day, let's get you showered and into some clean clothes." I stand up from the bench as I say this and walk into the house. Porter following closely behind. He goes into the bathroom, and I hear the shower turn on. I wait a few minutes in the kitchen, prepping the both of us a lunch for today and throwing some toast in the toaster for Porter.

"Are you going to come with me today to clean up the pool and hot tub?" I ask Porter as I hear the shower turn off. A few footsteps, the opening and closing of a cabinet and Porter opens the bathroom door, towel wrapped around him, nodding vigorously.

"Yes, I'm going with, I can help you clean and stuff too." He says this and smiles brightly up at me and walks to the clothing tub to pick out his outfit.

I turn back toward the kitchen just as the toast pops up from the toaster. I pull it out and put it on a plate next to a glass of water on the counter. I put both our lunches into a bag and set it on the counter before I finish cleaning up after myself in the kitchen.

Both of us ready to go, Porter having eaten his toast and drank his water, and myself with lunch and the office keys in hand, we head out the door.

Today shouldn't be too difficult a day as far as cleaning goes. I just need to check the filter on the hot tub and make sure there's not any new floaties in the pool, sweep around the pool and hot tub and take out the trash/clean surfaces in the recreation room.

Porter and I finish cleaning quickly, but before we leave, I go back into the recreation room and grab one of the random books we keep in here that people have left behind in the past. I toss it into the bag with our lunches and head back outside. I motion to Porter and we start walking toward the park when I look up and see Joe and Sadie walking towards us.

"Hi Joe!" I say and wave at the two of them. Porter smiles brightly and waves at them both as well.

"Hey kids! What are you guys getting into on this beautiful Saturday morning?" He and Sadie begin walking toward us.

"We just finished cleaning up the pool area and the recreation room, we're about to hang out at the park for a few, maybe play some games later." I say and look from Porter, grinning from cheek to cheek, back to Joe, who is smiling as well.

Sadie comes running up to us and I rub her head before she heads straight for Porter and gives him kisses upon kisses as he giggles and pets her head. He then sits on the ground, playing with Sadie as she snuggles up to him. I let out a giggle and look back to Joe who's laughing as well.

"Those two seem to be quite fond of each other." Joe says letting out a lighthearted laugh that fills the air around us.

"Would you guys like to join us at the park for a while?" I ask him this knowing there's no chance of Judith showing up if he agrees.

"We would love to, however I think Sadie and I are just going to head back to the house and maybe get a nap in. I truly appreciate the offer though, maybe next time." He says this as he pats me on the shoulder and then calls Sadie after him. He waves goodbye and we wave as well, watching as he walks toward his home and out of our view.

"Well kid, what would you like to do with the rest of our day? We don't have to go grocery shopping anymore this weekend, I managed to get everything we needed earlier this week, so it's whatever you want to do, we can stay at the park, or we can go somewhere else." I smile at Porter as he looks up in thought. He's got the cutest little face when he's thinking, one side of his face scrunched up with his lips pursed. He then relaxes his face in excitement like he just had an amazing thought. He does a half jump in excitement at his idea.

"Can we go to the water?" He says and does another small half jump. What he means by 'the water' is a small little pond at the public park that's about half a mile away from here. I smile down at him.

"Sure bud, that sounds perfect." Lunches in one hand and Porter's hand in the other, I start walking us toward the pond. It's a nice day today, warm yet not too warm. The closer it gets to summer the warmer every day is and the less rain we see each day. Porter will be starting summer break in a few weeks, and we'll have to go back to our summer schedule where he gets to go to work with me every day. Not super fun for him, yet I love it.

"Can we play some games when we get back to the house today, Stelly?" Porter asks as he walks next to me, happiness exuding in every step. This moment feels like utter bliss, the idea that Porter doesn't have to stress about anything, even for two days, I couldn't imagine anything better. Every time he's like this it just fills me with even more motivation to make sure I can figure a way out for us.

"I mean of course, just prepare to get your butt kicked." I wink and smile down at him, and he nudges my side. He's looking down at his feet, and I can still see the edge of his giddy smile.

We round the last corner to the pond and walk up to the picnic table closest to the water. I set down our lunches and sit on the bench and watch Porter start running around the grass with glee. He then walks up to the water and bends down just staring out for a few minutes before he gets back up and walks over to me.

Even if there wasn't a pond here, I think Porter would still like this area better. The 'park' in our little trailer neighborhood isn't really a park, we just call it that. It's more of just a small open grassy area in the center of the trailer park with one old, worn picnic table resting on a cement slab. So, it's not really a park, it's just the only grassy area in the community, people mostly use it as a shit box for their dogs and usually don't pick up after them. The area we're in now is a park, with a pond at the center. It's a big open space that Porter can run around in and play in the grass. He also loves to watch the ducks that live at this pond squawking and flapping around, sometimes we'll even give them bread so they come up to us. Porter has always loved any animal he has encountered and they usually love him right back.

I pull our sandwiches, two apples and two water bottles out of the brown paper bag that's sitting on the picnic table. I set Porter's lunch in front of him, and he begins to pull his sandwich out of its plastic bag. I usually try to reuse the plastic bags so we can save money on them. This is probably this bag's third or fourth use. I wash them and reuse them until the bag can't be used anymore.

I take my sandwich out as well and begin eating it, enjoying the simple pleasure of a PB&J in good company.

A few bites in I stop and pull the crust off of my sandwich, placing it on the plastic bag. Porter looks up at me excitedly knowing exactly what I was thinking and continues to do the same to his sandwich.

Once we finished eating, Porter and I look at each other grab our crusts and race toward the water. We both crouch down, closer to the water and I nod to him, and he pulls a small piece off the end and throws it in.

A few seconds later we see one of the pond ducks swimming toward us. It pecks at the soggy bread and then swallows it. It turns toward us and cocks its head. We laughed and I pull off a piece of my crust and toss it in the direction of the duck, but a little closer to the shore so it would have to get closer to us to get its treat.

"Do you think we'll be able to get it to come to us?" Porter says with hope glistening in his eyes.

"Maybe, we just have to stay relaxed and keep throwing the bread closer to us little by little." Porter nods vigorously, accepting the challenge and looks at the water with complete focus. He pulls off a piece of bread and goes for it, making it almost in the perfect spot. Excited, he is about to celebrate making his mark and then seems to remember we're trying to be calm. He settles back down and giggles in my direction. The duck doesn't notice Porter's movement and goes for the bread closer to us.

We continue like this until the duck is about four feet from us and Porter is on his last piece of bread. The duck looks up at us with curiosity, it almost seems like it's waiting for its next bite from us.

"What do I do now?" Porter asks in a whisper.

"Slowly reach your hand out with the bread and we'll just have to see if she approaches." I whispered back to him. He nods once and slowly reaches out his hand with the bread sticking out from the tips of his fingers. We both watch intently as the duck slowly moves closer little by little. She's watching us just as intently as we're watching her. When she's about a foot away from us, she quickly swims up and snatches the bread from his fingers before she swims away. We continue watching and right when she's almost out of sight she turns back and tilts her head once more as if to say thank you before she's on the other side of the pond.

"That was so cool!" Porter says in his normal voice now and jumps up from his crouching position. I stand up as well and we both start walking back to the table together.

"Can we do this every time we come here?" He says with excitement still written all over his face.

"Sure bud, that was a lot of fun." I say smiling at him. Porter is walking next to me with pure, unadulterated joy. His arms swing at his sides, and his smile lights up my world. This is one of those moments that I wish I could stay in forever. Unfortunately, I can't stop time, so instead I snap a picture of Porter in my mind so I can come back here whenever I want.

Chapter Six

It's Monday again. I brush my fingers across the wet morning dew that has built up into tiny little mountains on the picnic table outside the trailer. I feel the moisture soaking through my sweats where my thighs rest against the soggy wooden bench. The cold seeps through my legs and travels through my body like a cold breeze traveling through a forest.

The dark blue sky has slowly been growing brighter. Every minute that goes by with the sun becoming more and more brilliant, I can gradually feel my skin tingle with warmth until the sky has changed from dark to light and the cold only remains in the damp parts of my sweatpants.

Judith came back late last night, well technically very early this morning.

I felt her before I saw or heard her. The vibration of the car woke me from my fragile sleep as it pulled up, then it was the shake of the trailer when she landed on it's first shaky step. Next was the smell, the familiar yet overpowering scent of booze reached the inside of my nose through the door of the trailer.

When my eyes finally opened, I watched the still shadow from the car's headlights reflect the shape of the small window into the dark living room, her voice, only slightly muffled, echoed through the small space in front of me. The still shadow began to move and then fell away as the sound of the car grew quiet.

There was a bang on the door and then the unsteady sound of scraping against the latch until I finally heard the click unlocking the door, the creaking of the door as it opened and the unbalanced stomping. The door slammed followed by stumbling footsteps and irritable, angry grunts parroting through the small room, down the short hallway and into the bedroom in the back. The last noticeable noise was the flopping sound of a body hitting the bed. The house trembled slightly right before it went back to silence, darkness and the unmoving stillness of the morning.

The few minutes I have left to myself outside I spend journaling in my notebook. The side of my right hand rubs faintly against the soft, damp pages of the book that spends most of its life outside under the trailer. The hours spent in the humid air has added to its texture and heightened the smell of the paper wafting to my nose. The pen is light, airy and free flowing when I write about Porter, however my writing changes form, darkens and weighs down my pen and journal when I write about her.

The idea that she holds that much weight over me is terrifying and I don't know how to escape.

Yet.

I keep writing, going back and forth about ways I could save us, ways I could get us out if this. Every time, it goes back to *I'm almost eighteen.*

I've thought about all of it, I could tell someone, a teacher, I could tell Sara or even Joe, there's just too high of a risk that Porter and I would get separated. I've even thought about the fact that trying to keep us together is selfish because even if we were separated Porter could end up somewhere much safer and end up much happier, but there's always the downside of that as well, that he'd just be thrown into the system and end up somewhere just as bad, and without me. The guilt has been consuming me for years, not knowing what to do and not being able to do anything for Porter.

I had a chance once, when I got the scar on my face, the nurse that was tending to me was very suspicious of the nature of it. She waited until Judith wasn't around and asked me all kinds of questions about Judith, while also attempting to create a safe space for me to tell her all my deepest darkest secrets.

She had a soft face and a kind smile, I always felt love emanating off her like a warm hug. Every time she came to my room, she always made her presence known. There was always a deep pain in my chest to run into her warm embrace and let her hold me tight while I cried in her arms.

There was one morning, Judith had just left the room after repeating her fake smile and hidden threats of *you better not say anything, remember your brother is at home with me*, when Julie came in with her warm inviting smile and a vase of lilies. A week earlier she had asked me what my favorite flower was, I told her it was a lily, because to me Porter is my lily. Lilies, while they are beautiful on the outside they hold a sadness within, the meaning that always caught my eye was that they were meant to be a restoration of innocence to the souls of the dead. Porter continually restored my innocence and without him I thought my soul might as well be dead.

Julie placed the vase on the bedside table to my left and then gently sat down on the bed next to me. She radiated compassion, my eyes kept flickering back and forth between the lilies and her tenderness rapidly filling the room. In that moment with my symbol of Porter next to me and my growing trust in her, I almost told her everything. Then an image of Porter being ripped from my arms filled my mind and my words caught in my throat like a dry piece of bread with no water to wash it down. I stared at her for a moment and then swallowed hard as my secrets followed my saliva down to my stomach.

That was the last time I'd ever truly considered telling anyone and it was also when I decided to come up with a plan, so we could finally escape *together*.

The tingle of the air's cold breeze tickles my cheek as I slide my pen inside its elastic holder on the side of my journal. The hushed crinkle of the plastic bag under the trailer calls to me as I slide my journal into its cold pocket, zip it closed and sit back against the table's edge behind me. The birds gently end their morning chirps, alerting me to the end of my alone time this morning.

* * *

I can taste the metallic flavor of blood along with the burning sensation on my right cheek from the weight of her hand.

My head spins as the dizziness sets in. The room around me blurs and refocuses a few times. The world encasing me is muffled and then loud, back and forth nauseatingly repetitive.

I blink, her fuzzy figure is waving her arms around with what is probably a beer in her hand and her voice is running through my ears as if I'm underwater.

I blink again, she's somehow two feet closer and I can see her clearly this time.

"You stupid bitch, I fucking told you…" I blink again. Her voice fades to a low tone again swimming through jello and my vision, once again is clouded. I blink — she's clear — I blink — she's fuzzy. I feel my body trying to steady itself to no avail. There's a blur to my right and then a fiery pain against my temple — somehow I'm now on the floor smelling the rotting of the soggy brown carpet beneath me.

I lay there for what feels like forever, blinking over and over again, desperately trying to get my body to move. I feel the motions of Judith's anger on the floor that's still pressing against my body. I need to get up.

My head throbs as I lay there fighting my body's natural responses. Every motion causes my stomach to drop and my head to become even more woozy. Still, I keep pushing because I know what happens if I don't. It's me or him. How can I be so weak?

It's me or him.

Get up Stella! I yell to myself over and over!

Get up!

Get up!

GET UP!

I push myself forward on the floor crawling desperately toward Porter.

My eyes are wet, whether they're watering, or I'm crying, I can't tell. My vision is still blurry and the only thing keeping my body moving is the knowledge that I'm getting closer to Porter.

I reach what feels like his tiny toes and force myself to look up. Judith is towering above Porter who is helplessly curled up on the floor beneath her.

He has his arms wrapped around his head attempting to protect himself. From what I can tell she has been hitting his arms repeatedly with her fists trying to get him to react.

I struggle to get my body over the top of Porter's to cover him from any further blows. I feel him crumble beneath me.

"Pathetic! You fucking idiot!" I can tell she's directing this toward me. Before I can do anything she's kicking me again.

I'm okay with it, knowing Porter is safe beneath me.

"Ughhhhhh" She lets out a loud obnoxious sigh, "Oooo, big girl, you wanna protect *little* brother now huh?"

I can feel her spit landing on my back as she attempts to emphasize all her words. She steadies herself, preparing to start kicking me again.

It's still early in the morning and from how drunk she is, I'm guessing she brought a bottle into her bedroom when she first got back, and what I assumed was her sleeping was probably her drinking.

I can barely stay awake, yet I'm conscious enough to hear her walk to the couch. I manage to move my head just enough to see her.

She doesn't move and for a split second, it almost seems like there's a slight sadness in her eyes. Then in an instant it disappears, they lose their life and then the lids of her eyes shut.

I lay there frozen when I hear her body smack against the couch. Still covering Porter with my body we stay like that for a few more minutes. That is one of the weirdest things she's ever done.

Hearing no movement, I take a deep breath in after realizing I was holding it.

I hear a tiny whimper from beneath me and notice that Porter's body is shaking as he gasps for air between his wails, I feel the dampness of his tears begin to soak my shirt.

My chest begins to hurt, and I pull my arms around him and grip him as tight as my broken body can. I breathe in and as I breathe out, I feel a tear fall from my cheek.

"I'm so sorry, I'm so, so sorry." I repeat under my breath to Porter over and over. *I'm so sorry I haven't saved us*, I think to myself. *I'm so sorry for being selfish and not at least saving you, I'm so sorry I'm selfishly keeping us together and I'm so sorry I'm too weak to kill her myself. I'm so sorry Porter, I'm so sorry.*

Tears begin to stream down my face and into his curly blonde hair. I will save us Porter, I will.

The pain in my chest tightens, I grip Porter tighter and hold him as close as I can.

Every breath, my chest moves up and down, with each fall, my chest seems to tighten even more. Each intake of air becomes more and more shallow until the space between each breath is barely there and I am gripping Porter, gasping for air.

Porter pushes against me until his glassy brown eyes are looking up at me with concern. He pulls his arm free from my grip and places it against my cheek. His little hand is so soft and gentle, and it helps me to pull in a single full breath.

I can't force the pain away just yet, but his little touch still helps me to calm down and breathe.

"Stelly? It's okay Stelly, I love you, that's enough right?" His gentle soul amazes me, just the fact that he so quickly went from distress to concern for me. I sigh and realize that my breathing has steadied even more.

"Always kid, you always have and always will be enough for me. I love you so much Porter." I pull him in tighter and kiss his forehead, another tear falls from my cheek as I realize how incredibly lucky I truly am that I have been given such an amazing brother.

Chapter Seven

The handle to the front door silently slips out from under the tips of the fingers on my right hand back into its spot against the lock. Slowly I turn around and shoot Porter a smile of relief. He silently laughs and grins ear to ear.

Most of our morning we spent tiptoeing around Judith's scrunched body on the couch. We got ready as quickly as possible, managing to cover any upcoming bruising.

Swiftly moving from the door, I bump Porter playfully. And feel him giggle as I pull him to my side and start our walk to the bus stop. His small size six shoes dramatically stomp next to me as we walk creating a goofy dance with his feet. I pick up his rhythm and follow along with my own feet in his adorable, happy dance.

Laughing the whole way there, we eventually make it to the bus stop. Ending one of my many laughs this morning, I look down at Porter and let out a happy sigh.

"Well kid, we made it." I smile at him only slightly out of breath and enjoying every second of it.

"Yup! We did and we laughed the whole way!" He said through another giggle. "Stelly?"

His tone changed slightly. I nod. "Why is it so hard for some people to be happy? Like…why can't everyone just laugh like this?"

"That's a good question bud, one I wish I had the answer for, but what I know for sure is that I'm grateful to be able to laugh with you." I respond, my hand gently resting on his shoulder.

His bone pokes against my palm, I can feel the lack of nourishment in his body through my own badly nourished bones.

Guilt begins to slither its way up my throat one painstakingly slow gulp at a time. I shake my head dislodging the red serpent from my throat and let it fall back down to its home in the deepest darkest corner of my stomach.

The deep grumble of the school bus yanks me from my head and back to the present, back to my brother who stands there patiently with my hand still on his shoulder. I gently move my hand from his shoulder and pull him in for a hug.

He pulls away, winks at me with a goofy grin lingering on his face as he runs toward the yellow monster.

I stand there, feet planted in the middle of the sidewalk, and I enjoy this moment. The gentle breeze brushes my hair from my face pulling a small smile on my lips. Warmth brews in my chest and spreads throughout my body. A whisper of a smile and my entire being fills me with joy, what a miracle it is to have someone who loves you unconditionally.

I stay there a moment longer watching the bus drive away, the pungent fumes of the grey smoke it leaves behind fill my nose. Holding onto the bliss of the moment I turn away to start my walk home.

I stopped in my tracks, my arms and legs locked in place. It was as if my whole body was holding its breath.

Kaleb?

My eyes were locked on his green ones from across the street.

He's leaning up against his truck as if he was waiting for me to see him. He hesitated for a moment, like you would when you weren't sure if the dog you were approaching was gonna run or let you come closer.

His hesitation didn't last long because before I knew it he was already halfway across the street heading directly toward me. There was a smile on his face that could light up a football field. I almost feel like I'm drowning, my body is heavy, it feels like there's weights on my ankles locking me in place.

The last time I saw him he was dropping Porter and me off at 'home', the feeling was almost nostalgic, I didn't want to let it go, and felt like I had to.

Even though I decided I wasn't going to see him again, that it was too dangerous, I feel myself swimming in the nostalgia at the sight of him.

Just the knowledge we're about to be close enough to breathe the same air, I almost allow the hopeful air to swallow me. I suddenly feel sick, armored in shame and self-reproach. All these conflicting emotions are making me dizzy.

The breeze of his quick motions reach me before he does, bracing myself for his impact, he wraps his burly arms around me. His embrace breaks my rigid stature allowing my arms to hang loosely at my sides.

My body slumps into him releasing the tension it was holding onto so tightly only seconds ago.

I can tell he feels me let go because he only holds me tighter. For some reason that was reassuring, and I could feel my emotions creeping closer to my eyes. Before I could stop it, I let one tear seep from my eye. At that I quickly pulled myself away from him and subtly wiped my tear, so he didn't see.

"It's good to see you, Stel." He says and takes a half step backward now with a much gentler smile on his face.

"Yeah." Is about all I can muster, forcing a half smile onto my face.

At that moment I realize that the half smile actually wasn't forced at all. I want this, and I've *wanted* this, I want a friend and I don't want to fight it anymore.

"Yeah Kaleb, it's really good to see you too." I smile for real this time. As long as I'm careful, having him around could actually be a really good thing for both Porter and me. I can see by the reaction on Kaleb's face that he can tell I'm being sincere. I'm glad.

"Sooo does that mean you're gonna let me give you and Porter rides during the week?" He sends a cheeky grin my way. I roll my eyes with a smile on my face.

"I guess I will allow you to do us this extraordinary favor." I smile wider and gently smack his arm. He's unaffected, and unimpressed, looking down at his arm, he raises his eyes to me.

"Well, then I guess we should get going." He waves me toward his truck, when I don't move right away, "Don't tell me I'm gonna have to carry you to the truck again." He just starts laughing as I glare in his direction walking to his truck.

* * *

It's been about two weeks now that I've let Kaleb give us rides.

Porter was out of his mind excited when Kaleb and I pulled up to his school the first day and was just as excited the next morning when he picked us up at "home" as well.

The last two weeks have been so full of love and life and joy, it's almost unnerving. I'm having a hard time trusting that something horrible isn't waiting for me around the next corner.

Currently, Porter is sitting between Kaleb and me on the soft seat. Kaleb's cracking jokes back and forth with him.

When we pull up to the school, Kaleb reaches over and begins tickling Porter telling him he better hurry before the tickle monster keeps him here forever.

Porter is laughing uncontrollably, wiggling around like a worm and then accidentally pops Kaleb in his nose with his elbow.

Porter immediately shrinks back and suctions to my side, repeating over and over how sorry he is to Kaleb.

Kaleb is frozen in his seat and it's obvious by the look on his face he noticed the fear in Porter's eyes. Kaleb softens his face to a gentle smile, almost as if a wave of understanding has just washed over him.

"It's okay Porter, it was just a little bump." As he says this, he reaches over to Porter who is still attached to my hip, scrunches his hair and then slowly moves closer and wraps his arms around his tiny body in a reassuring hug.

"You're okay buddy." Kaleb leans back and reaches his hand out for Porter to take.

Porter grabs his much larger hand with his tiny one and lets him lead him out of the car. I watch from the passenger seat as the two of them walk to the front door before Porter separates from Kaleb and walks himself inside.

The truck shakes as Kaleb hops back into it next to me. I smile at him, appreciative that he's so gentle and kind with Porter. He seems to genuinely care for him.

"So, would you like to go get some breakfast with me?" Kaleb asks, his head tilted slightly as if to say please, and I can tell he's also nervous that I'm going to say no.

So many things run through my mind in this moment, how two weeks ago I would have been desperate to get home to get things done for the house before I had to get to work at ten, but today wasn't like that. I've had so much extra time with Kaleb giving us rides that there's actually not anything for me to do this morning before work. So, for the first time in a long time, I actually have some free time.

"Yes, I'd like that." Kaleb's eyes widen for a moment and then he relaxes and smiles at me almost mischievously.

"Then I know the perfect spot."

After about a fifteen minute drive, Kaleb is putting the truck in park and hopping out. I'm slightly confused because I don't see a restaurant anywhere, or even a bakery.

In front of us is just an empty parking lot surrounded by trees. Hesitantly I pull the handle to the door, but before I can open it all the way, Kaleb is pulling it open from outside. His hand is outstretched toward me as if it's telling me to 'come on!'

I grab his hand and let him pull me from the truck. His hand still gripping mine, he leads me around the end of the truck and toward the tree line. The closer we get; I can see that there's actually a small opening creating a path. We start our way down this path, wet leaves crunching under our shoes. My arm brushes up against a few branches, the wet rain still laying gently on them slightly dampens my jacket. A drop of morning dew falls from a tree above me and splashes on my nose. I look up and notice for the first time how beautiful it is here.

The trees moving together above me painting their own perfect canvas, sun shining through every other branch creating an alluring light show dancing through the shadows of the forest.

I realize I've stopped walking when Kaleb gently tugs my hand, I look back at him and keep following him down the path until it starts to widen more and more with every step.

In front of us now is not something I was expecting and it is absolutely beautiful. There's a small little cabin in the opening ahead of us. There are fairy lights strung from the cabin to the trees surrounding it. I notice a small sign just to the left of the door to the cabin, small enough you could miss it. The sign reads, 'The Faerie House'.

"What is this place?" I say as Kaleb smiles down at me.

"This is one of my favorite places for breakfast, it's kind of like a tea house/pastry shop/breakfast place. The best part to me is that they don't have any advertisements for it anywhere, all their business comes from word of mouth which is why there were no signs to get here, and their sign is so small out front too."

He goes on to explain a little more about how the owner really wanted people to have an experience good enough here that they couldn't help but tell other people. And that they've created just that, that they're actually quite a busy place and it's surprisingly slow right now, but he doesn't mind that because now I get to have my own experience. My face stretches into a smile that I send his way as I head toward the cute little cabin.

The front door makes a light creaking sound as I push it open. The inside of the cabin is lit up only by little fairy lights, although it's not dim at all because they are spread out through the cabin beautifully and they give the ambiance in here a warm welcoming yellow glow. The girl behind the counter smiles at me and welcomes me in. Her hair is black with bright blue tips, all pulled back in a short ponytail atop her head, her bangs hanging low in her face.

I notice how beautiful she is and in her own unique way. She's wearing black lipstick, but only light makeup everywhere else. The shirt hugging her upper half is a pale green with a mushroom in the center and she has an apron covering her lower half.

Something about this girl just screams confidence and I can feel myself envying her. I envy her freedom to be herself and the self-assurance she seems to have. I walk up to the counter and can feel Kaleb fill the space next to me.

"Well this is your favorite place, tell me what to get." I say to him and hope that he doesn't choose anything too expensive.

"You're right! You're just gonna have to let me surprise you then." He smirks at me, and I tilt my head slightly confused, how was he supposed to surprise me when I'm standing right here. He waves his hands at me like he's shewing me.

"Go on now, go look around the shop or go outside, it won't be a surprise if you're standing there." He says as if he just read my mind, but it's kind of obvious now that he's said it out loud. My cheeks get warm as I let out an embarrassed giggle and walk away.

I head around the corner and notice there's some seating inside around the back of the cabin, which makes sense because of how much it rains here. The tables and chairs in here are all unique, no matching sets or monotonous colors, each seating place has its own individuality just like the girl at the register. To my right is a white and yellow bistro set in the small corner, it's obviously vintage with bright yellow leather swivel chairs. Then on the left wall there's a wicker table and chair set which some people may have thought was meant for outside but somehow fits perfectly in here.

It is extraordinary here, like a dream. There were shelves on the walls with all kinds of homemade things for sale, soaps, lotions and also little figurines.

In the back corner there's a bright white table with red birds all over it and the chairs as well.

I find a table for us and sit down. I choose the seat in the corner with my back up against the wall so I can see when people are coming and going.

Not long after I sit down Kaleb comes walking around the corner with two teacups in his hands. He hands me mine and sits down.

"They make all their teas in-house, this is one of my favorites, it's a hibiscus berry tea, you don't even have to add sugar and it has a sweet flavor to it." I take a sip and smile at him.

"This is delicious!" I mean it too, this is probably the best tea I've ever had.

Especially seeing how most of my variety of tea tasting consisted of Lipton.

We both are sitting there just enjoying our tea as we wait for the food to come out. The kitchen door ahead of me to the right, gently swings open and the girl from the front desk walks toward us gracefully, yet confident with our food in hand. She places it on the table, lets us know to come get her if we need anything, smiles and walks away swinging her hips.

I look down at the feast in front of us. The smell was a mix of sweet and savory. On the table was a steaming brothy soup with what looked like melted cheese and soggy bread on top, to the left of that was a leafy salad with a chicken salad laying on the right side of the leaves. To the right of the soup were three mini scones and maybe whipped cream in a small bowl next to them and then randomly placed around the small dishes were mini desserts.

I started with the soup, and just as Kaleb instructed, I added a scoop of the melted cheese and soaked bread to the spoon filled with the dark brown broth and sliced onions. The flavors all hit my mouth at once like an explosion, it was sweet, tangy, and savory in one bite. Somehow the sogginess of the bread perfectly complemented the soft onions and stringy melty cheese. Then the base itself held the saltiness of a broth yet the caramel flavor of an onion.

"What is this?" I look at him amazed.

"French onion soup." He chuckles at my amazement.

I have never tasted anything like this before and I begin to allow myself to enjoy this until Porter's face pops into my mind. Once again, my body aches with guilt, but instead of ruining this moment for myself I decide to change my patterns this time.

"Kaleb?"

"Yes?" He looks at me, head tilted, but as always with a smile on his face.

"Can we please take Porter here? He would love it so much." My throat squeezes as I ask him this and for some reason my eyes get warm, and it feels like they are about to begin watering my cheeks.

I feel the tightening of my throat as I realize how nervous I am to ask him this. But the fear of anything negative instantly washes away when his smile warms my cheeks and softens my throat. I gulp and allow myself to be softened more and more by his kind and gentle being.

"Of course, Stel, I would love to show him this place." He says, and I instantly look away because for some reason there is a small water droplet swimming down my cheek from my eye. I gently wipe my eye and sit there for a moment attempting to make sense of this feeling. This intense feeling of...

What is it?

I haven't felt it in so long...

"I'm grateful to you Kaleb, thank you." I remember the feeling as soon as I say it. It's different from the gratitude I feel for Porter, it's almost like an untethered gratitude.

I'm grateful to Porter because we have each other in the hard times, and we create good. This moment felt like pure good, there was no negative.

There was nothing that Kaleb was running from with me, there was no desperation to stick together, he was just choosing to be here with me.

He was just genuinely good. That's what it felt like anyway in this moment. But I need to find out more about why he came back and why he's trying so hard to be in my life again.

"Why did you come back?" I glance at him quickly and then down at my hands resting on the table.

"Well, there's not much to it, I graduated from high school a few years ago, tried the college thing, it wasn't for me and then about six months ago, my uncle offered to mentor me working here at his mechanics shop so that one day I can take it over. I've been here since, just working on cars and attempting to set myself up properly."

He went on to explain that when he first got here his uncle also gave him his truck, which at the time was pretty much a parts car and his uncle told him that if he fixed it up, he could have it. When he first moved here he stayed with his uncle until he saved up enough to get his own place, he told me it was only a small studio apartment but that it was plenty for him. He told me a little more about his every day and that he doesn't start at the shop until ten which is how he can give us rides and he is also able to leave for a little in the afternoons to pick us up and just go back to what he was working on that day after dropping us off.

He seems like he's about to keep going but then his face changes and his shoulders drop, he looks at me with sadness encasing his being.

"I'm sorry I didn't say goodbye Stel, I've regretted that for a long time and have wished we could have stayed in touch."

I'm shocked that he's apologizing, I didn't think he even remembered. I hadn't realized how much I wanted to hear that until he said it, however it's a good thing he didn't try and stay in touch, I wouldn't have been able to anyway.

"I forgive you." I say this so quickly and I honestly didn't notice I meant it until it came out of my mouth. "Besides, you're not the only one who left." My words trail off and I feel myself filling with mixed emotions again, anger, disappointment, confusion.

"What do you mean Stel?" Kaleb looks at me with a sad sort of curiosity until sadness rests completely as if he realizes the answer to his own question. "Your dad?" My eyes widen and I recoil my head slightly.

"How did you know?" I'm sure my shock is obvious to him based on how wide my eyes got and how quickly my body shifted away from his response.

"It took me a few seconds, but I kind of figured because about a year after my dad and I left town, your dad stopped reaching out to us as well."

Apparently a few weeks before he stopped talking to them he told Paul that things had been rough with Judith and that he thought he might need to get away for a while to clear his head. A couple weeks later after that John completely stopped reaching out altogether. Paul tried reaching out for a while, he was super worried, and he called John's parents and they said John had done the same thing to them. After almost a year of no response, Paul figured their friendship just died out and he stopped calling.

The idea that my dad ghosted Paul completely blew my mind because of how close they were, but I guess it's not that surprising if he was willing to leave us.

Kaleb and I talk for a while longer until it's time for both of us to get to work. After having a real conversation with him pretty much for the first time since I saw him again we got to catch up and I told him as much about my current life as I could, but I could not get my dad out of my mind.

It was almost as if this new information was scratching an itch in my mind that hadn't been scratched in years. I couldn't put my finger on it, but something about the way my dad left just didn't feel right.

Chapter Eight

We'd been home for a few hours at this point, no sign of Judith yet, which was nice but also had me on the edge of my seat.

I can never quite relax all the way unless I'm not home or it's the weekend and I know she's gone.

Earlier this week I bought Porter and I a puzzle at a used bookstore for only a dollar and tonight Porter pulled it out from under the couch and is currently working on it in the middle of the living room floor.

There's a few times that I almost pulled myself out of my ready for anything position to crouch on the floor with him and work on this underwater picture piece by piece, but I couldn't. I just kept getting this feeling that something was coming so I've spent most of this evening on the edge of the couch with my eyes locked on the window and the front door.

Ever since we started spending time with Kaleb, Porter has slowly been acting more and more like a kid and I've loved it, but at times I feel like I have to be even more attentive and alert because of it. Either way I'm okay with that because his only job should be to be a kid.

I see Porter flinch at the same time as I hear tires screech outside and then the sound of laughter as two car doors open and close.

I quickly jump to the floor and in one swipe completely destroy Porter's creation and start throwing the little pieces back into their box. For a split second I allow myself to look at his face and I see nothing but focus as he helps me put the puzzle away. I'm glad he understands.

I'm shoving the puzzle box under the couch right as the front steps begin to shake and the loud obnoxious laughter is entering into our space.

I look at Porter and he is sitting behind me on the couch, I can tell that he's trying to hide his smaller body behind my own small body. I sit there rigid, ready for anything, ready to put on whatever face I need to lessen the pain for both of us.

Judith stumbles through the door first and in tow is some washed up band guy. He has shoulder length, dark brown greying hair that's slicked back with grease into a short ponytail. His face is sparkled with grey and brown shorter hair creating a salt and pepper beard that sort of shapes his face however is obviously not well taken care of. He's wearing a dirty white long-sleeved shirt with a black leather vest over the top and black jeans that are much too tight for his body. There's a noisy silver chain hanging from one of the belt loops on his jeans and into his front right pocket that moves left to right as the two of them walk into the house. Out of nowhere he looks at me and then smacks Judith's butt.

"Stop it Gerry!" Judith says playfully to him and then pushes him away, biting her lip. I recoil in disgust and then Judith looks at me so I quickly hide my expression. "You two, get out." She says waving us toward the door.

"Oh, c'mon sweetheart they can stay." Gerry says this and I fight the growing urge to vomit as he looks me up and down licking his lips. Judith just rolls her eyes, scoffs, and drags him into her bedroom.

I grab Porter and pull us out of the house. Luckily, I put a book for us in a bag taped under the picnic table for a time just like this. I quickly stop and swipe the book from under the trailer and start running with Porter in tow, his hand in mine.

I keep running until we make it to one of our favorite spots under the big oak tree in the "park". The grass beneath the big tree is barely lit with light from the surrounding streetlights, but it's lit just enough, almost as if there's a spotlight just for us. I force air in, filling my lungs and breathe out, I'm able to relax my body again from the short run.

The tree in front of us looks almost as if it grew special for our reading time. The base of the trunk is about five feet wide and the area facing me is indented just enough for me to crawl into the tree, almost like it's wrapping its arms around me. Bending down, I sit in the tree's pocket. It's cold at first against my back but gradually grows to warm my body. I sit with my knees up but slightly apart so Porter can squeeze in and lay back on me while I read. I place the book on one of my knees and wrap my arms around Porter to reach the book in front of both of us.

My hand runs across the cover of the book, feeling the edges carved into it to create the title, as well as the many blemishes, caused by years of wear and tear and passing it down to new people.

As I read there's a part of me that separates from my reading self and this part of me gets lost in thought. I think about Porter's gentle breath moving up and down against my chest, his hands fidgeting in his lap, and I notice a new kind of gratitude for Porter, the kind of gratitude I felt this morning when I was with Kaleb.

My chest instantly begins to warm and I can feel a gentle smile change the structure of my face, but also slightly alter the tone in my voice as I read. I pause my reading only for a moment so that I can bend down and kiss the top of Porter's head and then go right back to the book.

Porter nudges his body closer to me and I gently squeeze him with my arms.

I recognize the shitty rusted car that was parked in front of the house speeding past us and exiting the park. I let out a huge sigh and nudge a sleeping Porter who has completely surrendered to exhaustion and is slumped against my chest and knee.

Slowly he pulls his head off my knee making it seem like it's thirty pounds and then turns his head about halfway to meet my gaze. He's got one eye about half open and his other almost looks like he's trying to squint out some dirt.

I let out a small giggle enjoying every part of this adorable moment. It seems that Porter notices my smile because he pushes a big ass grin even out of this sleepy face.

"Alright bud, let's go get you to bed." I pull myself free from underneath him and crouch down in front of him instead. "C'mon bud jump on." I motion for him to climb on my back, and he does.

I stand up, he's just barely small enough for me to carry him anymore, it's getting to the point that I struggle quite a bit and I do it anyway.

I feel a wave of gratitude wash over me at the thought that he's still so young. That he'll still be so young when I can get us out of here, that he'll still have so much life left to live that's not this hell.

When we walk up to the house, I put Porter down and walk closer to see if I can hear what the situation is in the trailer. I can hear the sloshing and clanking of a glass liquor bottle and some mumbling that I can't quite decipher.

It seems like she's in a pretty docile drunk mood, drunk enough to be angry, but fucked up enough that she won't move a whole lot. She's probably on her second bottle now.

"I'm gonna go in first, you sneak in behind me and get into your spot behind the couch, okay? You'll be okay, I got you." I gently rub his shoulder in an attempt to reassure him.

Porter is now wide awake which I knew would happen, but I tried to keep him sleepy anyway. He gives me one solid nod and I take that as my cue to go ahead.

I slowly pull the door open and brace myself for anything. Judith is leaning against the counter in the kitchen, the clear bottle of vodka in her hand is loosely spinning around almost like she's trying to stir the pungent liquid.

She looks up and it seems I've startled her because she flinches and her fingers slip a little further up the neck of the bottle. It takes a moment, but she steadies herself and eventually she's rolling her eyes and looks at me like she just ate something foul. I feel my body calming ever so slightly, it seems like she's merely irritated at the sight of me, which is much better than angry or furious.

The only thing I should expect from her tonight is to be treated like she doesn't like me, especially because of how fucked up she is tonight, she's barely even standing.

"You knooww you should reellly announce yoursewf, I almost dropped my BOTtle!" She slurs at me slightly yelling the beginning of the word bottle.

She sounds just like a toddler throwing a tantrum over spilled milk. Not something to fear, but definitely wary of.

"That's my bad, I didn't intend to startle you." My voice is flat and emotionless, she's so out of it I could care less about faking anything, she's not going to notice.

Judith scoffs, wobbling in a weird circle to place the bottle in her hand on the counter behind her, as soon as she does. I hear small quiet footsteps quickly pass behind me and then stop.

I make no indication that I heard Porter pass behind me, I'm not stupid enough to give him away. Judith 'quickly' turns back around and squints her eyes at me, I stare back at her with a blank expression still unmoving and hopefully keeping her attention directed to where I'm standing in the small entryway of the trailer.

"--idyou earr that?" Her eyes still locked on me.

"Hear what?" I say once again with no tone changes or interest in my voice.

"Whatever, where's the ovveer 'ittle monster I barfed—birfed?" I take no time to pause or think of what I should say.

"Not here."

Eye roll.

"Okayyy wellll I foought you bof might want to know that I'm going away" burps "with Ger–Gerry, I'm sure you could tell but he's… in a… BAnnd. Anyways, he's got a gig in Vegas and I'm going! Le–leaving tomorroww."

I can't control my body as my eyes slightly widen, it's just that this actually surprises me.

All of a sudden, my thoughts are moving a mile a minute, I can barely focus, still I force myself to come back to this moment. I need to know exactly what this means and how much time we'll have. I take a breath and bring myself back to a centered space where I can respond to her calmly.

"How long will you guys be gone?" She rolls her eyes again and then glares at me through squinted eyes. She looks at me like the question I asked was not only stupid but also annoying.

"I don't FUckin–ing know Stellrrr, probably like a month? Mayybe sic week or somefing, why do you cARe? it'll be a whiiille."

Something similar to relief maybe, filled my body, my chest tightened and then released at the same time, it was almost like I was suffocating and all of a sudden, the room filled with oxygen again.

"Yo–U twoo shits will be fiiine." And that was it, I stood there breathing for the first time, yet somehow also breathless watching her drag herself away from me and into her bedroom for the night.

A month.

My birthday is in four months.

A month with her not even in the same state is so much time that I could start prepping to set myself up for us to get away. I can look for apartments and work more hours, I could even maybe look for some odd jobs around town. I notice that I am now facing the complete opposite direction and my eyes are locked on Porter who is poking his head out from behind the couch. He has an unsure smile on his face like he's not sure if he should be excited or not yet.

I send a nod his way and I can see the look of relief on his face that I just felt myself. I take two big steps toward him, crouch down and swiftly pull him into my arms confirming his sense of ease once again.

We're going to make it Porter, we're getting out of here.
I WILL save us.

Chapter Nine

My eyes open swiftly.

I scan the room; I don't remember falling asleep. My arm feels heavy, I look down and see a sleeping Porter suctioned to my side. My body aches slightly from being stuck in the same position all night.

It's not the most comfortable, and I don't care. I still have about thirty minutes before I need to get up, so I stay there, muscles cramping and allow Porter to continue sleeping.

Gently I brush the back side of my hand against Porter's soft baby face. His eyes flutter open and when he sees me his eyes widen in bliss.

"We get a month Stelly." He whispers and I know that even if I wasn't looking at him, I'd be able to hear that beautiful smile in his voice.

It's almost too good to be true, this could end up being one of the best months we've had in a while. I catch myself feeling hopeful again but this time it's not the complete feeling, it's mixed with fear. As if there's this lingering feeling of, just wait, you're not safe yet.

The morning goes by quickly and we're about to head out the door to meet Kaleb at "our house" when all of a sudden, there's a knock at the door.

Instantly my eyes widen in a panic and I scurry to the window to see who it is.

No, no, no, no, no, how did he find this place?! There were obvious signs of panic and fear on my face because it reflected in Porter's.

Quickly I motion for Porter to go hide in his spot, I'm rushing to the door hoping that I'm quick enough and he doesn't knock again, but here's to hope because there it was again. I swing the door open swiftly and quietly shut it behind me.

I grab Kaleb and start pushing him away from the door focused on getting him to his truck. He doesn't let me push him very far.

He has planted his feet firmly in where he stands, still way too much in the open for my comfort.

"What are you doing here?!" I shout-whisper to him and then I shake my head because it doesn't matter he just needs to leave.

"Kaleb you have to go, right now!" I say this and attempt to push him away again. He grabs my hands to comfort me. I rip them away.

"Huh? Stel, you don't have to be embarrassed that you live in a trailer park, I don't care about that stuff, I just want to hel–"

"What?! No! Kaleb that's not it, I can't explain it right now! You just have to go, you have to leave, *please*."

I didn't try to force him away this time I just tried to plead with him with my face hoping that maybe that would work. He still looked confused, but his face softened slightly and he seemed to concede as he gently tapped me on the head and then turned around and started toward his truck. I sigh in relief that I won this battle and hope that she didn't wake from his knocking.

Unfortunately, it was too late.

I hear scuffling from inside and then Porter talking softly and I realize in that moment how stupid I am, of course he's going to try and stop her. Porter's a smart kid and it doesn't surprise me in the least that he caught on to the situation. In addition to Porter's voice, there's a thud and then her voice.

Fuck. I know those sounds all too well. I rush to the door to come to Porter's rescue and before I can open the door it swings open grazing my nose and smacks loudly against the outside of the trailer. If Kaleb hadn't already turned back around, I'm sure he would now, and I can't even take the time to look back and check because the monster is out and it's my job to slay it.

"What is going on here *Stella*?!" She spits my name like it's venom. I know for sure now that Kaleb is still here because Judith keeps looking behind me and then back at me over and over.

I can tell that she's trying very hard to hold back because we do currently have an audience, but she's not very good at pretending when she's in the beginning of a rage.

I'm about to respond when I hear his voice behind me. *Fuck, fuck, no! Just get in your truck and go! You're just making it worse.*

"-- apologies, I only meant to help, this is on me not Stella, I didn't mean to intrude." I drown out my thoughts enough to hear Kaleb try and smooth things over, it obviously doesn't work.

"Stella, who the fuck is this?" Judith completely ignores Kaleb and looks directly at me in disgust.

"Judith, it's me, Kaleb, I understand why you might not recognize me, I have changed a lot over the years." He says this so kindly and so *stupidly* too, what is he thinking right now?!

My eyes are locked on Judith and for a moment I think I see something that looks like a spark of recognition, it fades so quickly I can't quite tell. Her eyes lock back on me.

"He's no one, he's just some guy that was checking out the park the other day and I guess he figured out what trailer I was in, I'm guessing he's just stopping by to ask a question." I shrug and look back at Kaleb and I see him for the first time since Judith came out here and his face is wrecked with pain.

I can feel his hurt and confusion from here. I want to run to him and allow him to hold me... I just can't.

"*Lies!*" Judith spits at me, just barely loud enough for me to hear. "I'm not sure who this kid is Stella. You brought him here and you need to get rid of him *now.*"

I can feel Kaleb's eyes pouring into my back and it was that feeling that got me to notice Judith's grip on my arm, nails digging in.

"I'm sorry, now's really not a good time, you need to leave." I say this after I've turned to look at Kaleb and when his eyes meet mine, it feels like regret I see in them. It was only for a moment though. Kaleb straightens his back and switches to look at Judith. He begins to take quick steps toward me and Judith and I start shaking my head begging him to just leave.

He doesn't.

Before I can say anything, he's pushing his own arm between me and Judith. I'm now standing behind his large body watching in horror at what's playing out in front of me.

"No. I'm sorry," he glances back at me, "I shouldn't have just shown up, but Judith is everything alright? You seem out of it. Are you okay?"

She's going to think he's mocking her and that's not going to play out well for us.

"Kaleb, please just go, you're just making it worse."

Kaleb looks back at me and then toward the trailer, when we both see Porter behind Judith with tears streaming from his face. He looks as if he's pleading with him too.

I hear a sigh escape from the large body in front of me.

"It doesn't seem like this is going anywhere, however Judith, I need you to know that I know. You will be seeing me again." He glares at her and then looks at me.

I'm visibly shaking as he puts his hands on my shoulders, his eyes locked on mine. I want to look at him, however I keep fluttering my glance to Porter and then back to Kaleb. I can't focus on him right now.

"Stel, please, if you need me, I won't be far away. Like right around the corner, all you have to do is call and I'm right there." I can't stand it anymore.

I push him away and run toward Porter.

"Just go Kaleb, we'll be okay." I don't even glance back at him when I say this.

As soon as I'm close enough Judith is sending daggers toward Kaleb and ripping me into the trailer, her nails digging into my upper arm again. As soon as the door shuts behind her, she throws me to the floor.

"You selfish piece of garbage. I tell you I'm leaving, and you think you can just bring people over now?"

She laughs maniacally and reaches down to grip my shirt. Her face is now inches from mine, scrunched and tensed in anger almost as if she was holding something in and shooting hatred at me with every ounce of energy in her body. Her jaw is clenched and she's gripping tight enough to rip my shirt. She shakes me once and then tosses me backward.

"God, I fucking *hate* you." She spits at me, filling the air with the hot, dense loathing she has for me. "Truly I wish you were never born, the sight of you disgusts me." She looks away from me and then as if her body is suddenly triggered, she slightly jerks her body to the left and then her right hand is swinging toward me in a quick steady motion.

As if in slow motion I feel the bones in the back of her right-hand crush into my cheek. It's almost as if I could feel each knuckle landing in a different place. I feel the sting first, it sticks around until my cheek fills with the heat of pain instead. It then turns into a throbbing numbness that spreads through the right side of my face. The throbbing is almost more excruciating than the pain because of how it spreads through not just my cheek but to my eyesight and my hearing.

Judith is once again standing over me and this time instead of disgust she has a satisfied disturbed grin spreading from cheek to cheek. Her feet begin landing blows in my side, my stomach, my legs. I feel myself grasping at consciousness when I hear Porter yell.

He's begging her to stop. Her kicking stops and I take a moment to grasp my reality and pull myself up from the floor into a sitting position. And that's when I first notice that in all the commotion of the morning, mine and Porter's clothing tub didn't get completely pushed back under the couch and now Judith was facing exactly in the direction of it. Panic sets in and adds to the pain ravaging my body, my chest is squeezing tight just hoping that my luck is not this bad and that she doesn't notice the tub.

Her body is rigid looking at Porter, his eyes are filled with fear and before I'm even sure of what's happening Judith is slowly turning her body toward me again. She is once again smiling at me with suspicion spread all across her face.

"What's that Stella?" My heart sinks as I realize that this past year and a half of hard work has now been wasted. How could I have been so stupid?? I knew I should have moved my stupid stash, I could have buried it outside, hidden it in the office or so many other places! Why was I not more careful?!

She's right. I am a piece of garbage.

Judith doesn't wait for me to respond. She pushes Porter out of the way, onto the floor as she makes her way closer to our escape.

I'm praying that by some chance she pulls the tub out, sees only clothes, and doesn't look any further.

My prayers go unanswered as I watch through blurry eyes as she starts pulling all of our savings out of the tub. A greedy smile spreads across her face.

I jump up from the floor and push her as hard as I can.

She falls against the side of the couch.

I quickly grab for the money in her hands while she struggles to get herself off the floor. I feel a few bills rip between our hands and I know immediately that this infuriates her even more.

I back up with some of the cash, luckily Porter has already snuck into his spot.

Judith finally pushes herself up from the dirty carpet. Before I can react, she's swinging at me. Her hand bashes the side of my head.

I'm falling to the ground and my head hits the floor.

The world fades to black.

* * *

My eyes open and my head begins to throb.

I notice my hand gripping something in front of me and when I open my palm I see the corner piece of a ten-dollar bill.

Time goes by as if in fast forward. My chest is tight and it's almost impossible to fill my lungs with air. Oxygen enters my body through small little gasps every few seconds. All motion in front of me is blurred and begins to create streaked images of colors in front of me. I feel like I'm disappearing.

Slowly.

Gently.

Fading.

It's over.

That was my plan. I have no idea how I can get the both of us out of this anymore. It's almost ironic how it only takes thirty minutes for our entire future to vanish. How easy. How fucking effortless she stole our freedom.

I'm done.

"Stelly?" I blink a few times and focus in on Porter bent down in front of me.

Stupid, stupid, you CAN'T give up.

"I'm here." I croak out, of course I'm here, I could never leave him.

"What are we gonna do Stelly?" I realize now how panicked Porter really is.

"She took all of it and it's my fault! I didn't push the tub in all the way!" Porter is now wailing in front of me, tears washing his face.

"No!" I say sternly, Porter gulps and sniffles back his next set of wails. "This is NOT your fault Porter, don't say that again."

I tug him into my arms and almost instantly regret it when I feel pain shoot all over the parts of my body where he's now leaning on me.

I hold him against me in spite of the pain knowing it's what he needs right now. "Porter, I will fix this, we will be okay."

I slowly move myself out from underneath Porter and lay down on the couch knowing that my body needed rest. Porter climbs up onto the couch and wiggles into the empty pocket on my left side.

I close my eyes and give myself permission to drift off.

Chapter Ten

I *walk in the door of my family's small, cozy house and see my mom standing at the stove making us some sort of dinner.*

She has a cute little pink and white flowery apron on. Her hands start moving, chopping at some vegetables with grace, like a surgeon cutting into their patient. I ask her what she's making, she only smiles and says it's a surprise. Laughing into the living room, I see my dad sitting on the couch with a newspaper chuckling. I laugh again knowing that he's only reading the comics.

I walk to the back of the house and see a small bedroom filled with my things and new things I don't recognize, and somehow all things I like. On the back wall is a big window that stretches outside the walls. On each side of the window is a shelf filled with all my favorite books. There is a couch-like bench just under the window and between the shelves. I walk up to the bench and run my fingers across the soft white pillows laying against the back of the bench.

On the left side of the room is a bed I don't recognize with a white comforter laying on top and a small red throw pillow sloppily strewn across its surface. I then look down at the floor and my handwriting is all over the black painted floor in silver sharpie. It's filled with my handwriting, what looks like poems maybe? Some poems and lyrics written by others and some I don't recognize and yet somehow feel familiar. It's like the floor is made up of my handwriting. I start to read them, there are lots of poems about positivity and resilience. After a few minutes of reading, I notice something odd, 'I shouldn't… And yet I do, I love him.' My eyebrows scrunch together, who am I writing about?

I hear a breath behind me and turn around to see Porter standing in my doorway. He is very handsome for a little guy, and he looks beyond healthy. He just stares at me for a few seconds with a growing grin on his face, not a worry to be detected.

"Whatcha doin Stelly?" He says cheerfully.

"Not much really, just going over some of my writing." I say and smile back at him. His happy, happy smile fills me with joy.

"I see that you are in the Kaleb corner." He gives me a smirk and then winks.

"The what?" I laugh, slightly confused.

"Wow, Stelly, you must really miss him if you're that delusional. You know, it's your little corner of the floor that you have dedicated solely to writing about Kaleb?" Well, that answers my question. He laughs and stares at me looking slightly worried at my confusion. I quickly snap out of it and play along.

"Oh yeah, well of course I know what you're talking about, just spacing out."

I smile and stand up. When I reach him, I ruffle his hair a little. I then realized what else was so different about him. He's tall! Porter, my little brother, is almost taller than me. It's like he grew overnight. I laugh a little and walk into the bathroom that is just down the hall from my room.

Somehow, I can tell right away that Porter and I share this bathroom. He has all kinds of boy things, like boy deodorants and such on one side of the bathroom where as on my side I have one bottle of perfume and lotions and a very little amount of makeup and then other daily things a girl would use.

We both not only have our own sides of the bathroom, but our own sinks. On his side is a big open shower that basically opens to the rest of the bathroom. It has a curtain that's tucked behind a hook and doesn't look like it's used too often. On my side of the bathroom though, there is a jacuzzi bathtub. I take in a big breath of pure happiness.

Walking over to the bathtub I turn on the hot water and let it fill up while I look through my drawers and cabinets, looking for some sort of bath salts or something. When I open the bottom drawer on the left side I find a huge stash of relaxing bath stuff, like bubbles, salts, scrubs, etc. I grab the salts that say relaxation on them and throw some into the bath. Once the tub is filled all *the way I go to my room and pick a book. Once set with my book I get into the tub and start reading.*

I spend a while in the tub before I throw on some leggings and a t-shirt. I walk into the living room and see Porter sitting with my dad, who is in the exact same spot as before, newspaper still in hand. God knows how many times he read each comic. They just sit talking and laughing, just as father and son should. I walk over and sit on the ground in front of them.

"What're you guys talking about?" I ask, curious.

"Oh, we're just laughing at Porter's baseball coach again. He apparently started yelling at Tim today, one of Porter's teammates, because he made some sort of comment that offended him in some way. Which, to make comments like that at his age is totally normal and is no reason to get yelled at unless having said it directly to someone in a bullying manner, anyway."

My dad cut himself off with a laugh. He started on a new subject, about life, things a normal family would talk about. I just smiled, filled with joy. After a few minutes of listening to my dad jabber on and Porter sitting there and nodding his head slightly bored,

I hear a knock at the door. I start to get up when I hear my mom yell from the kitchen, "I got it!" I sit back down until I hear my mom again as she yells, "it's Kaleb hun!" And after about two seconds when I don't appear in front of her she walks around the corner almost running into me as I was on my way to the door and accidentally yells in my face,

"Stella your boyfriend is-" she gradually cuts herself off and laughs with me. I jump from being startled and she just tilts her head confused for a split second, then continues with a smile. "Your boyfriend is here." She says in a normal voice and laughs at herself with a slight sigh.

Walking past her, I see Kaleb standing in the doorway smiling with flowers.

"What are these for?" I smile and take the flowers from him.

"Just cause." He shrugs smiling and slides in for a kiss. I kiss him back and then pull away and look at him.

"Aww- how sweet." I say almost sarcastically with a big grin on my face as I walk into the kitchen and grab a vase under the sink for the flowers. I grab the scissors from the drawer where all the utensils that don't have an exact place go and start cutting flowers. When I'm about two flowers in, Kaleb comes up behind me and wraps his hands around my waist in a loose hug.

He watches me as I cut the ends at an angle. I don't exactly remember why you're supposed to do that. I giggle a little as Kaleb's hand tickles my waist. Once I'm done Kaleb moves back so I can fill the vase up with water and put the flowers out.

Kaleb grabs my hand and starts leading me out the door.

"Bye mom! Bye dad!" I yell back to them. Porter just nods at me as his way of saying goodbye. I roll my eyes.

"I love you too kid" I say and he just responds with another nod and a 'yeah, yeah'.

"So where are we going?" I ask Kaleb once we're outside heading to the car.

"Hmmm I'm not sure, where do you want to go? " He asks with a cheeky grin.

"Mmmmm I don't know, maybe go somewhere to see the stars and make out in the back of your truck?" I say grinning at him playfully.

He just smiles and opens my door for me. "Yes ma'am." He says and shuts my door, walking over to his side and getting in. "I like that idea."

Kaleb heads in the direction of the park that we always go to that has a very large open field that allows him to park his truck in the middle of it at night. I glance over at him, and I notice how perfect he really is for me. His arms are fit, not to the point of being too much though, he's tall and lean. His hair is light brown, complimenting his green eyes. His face is chiseled with sharp and soft features at the same time. Even so, his looks aren't all of it, I can feel his love for me from the other side of the truck.

"I love you, Kaleb." I say, getting a sudden feeling that I'll never have the chance to say it again. He looks over at me and laughs a little, smiling too.

"I love you too, babe. What brought that on?" He asks, honestly curious.

"Oh, you know just staring at you." I tease him. He just laughs at me and turns his focus back to traffic. I notice he has a phone jack to listen to music so I plug my phone in and shuffle a *playlist. Surprisingly he knows almost every song and we sing along together. We go on like this, song after song, until we get to the field where he drives into the middle.*

He puts his hand on my arm before I excit the cab.

"I have something for you." He looks up at me and then to his left pulling something out from the side pocket of the truck. It's a small picture frame with a painting inside of me reading by myself.

"Wha—" I look up at him smiling. The painting was beautiful. "When did you paint this? It's beautiful!" I pull him in and quickly kiss his lips before looking back to the painting.

"Not as beautiful as you." He winks at me before he ushers me to follow him out of the truck.

I jump out of the cab and meet him behind his truck. He's holding the blankets he leaves in his car for nights like this. I open the tailgate and jump in, he hands me the blankets and I start laying them out in the bed of his truck, leaving one of the five super thick fuzzy blankets out to put over us when we lay down. He jumps up into the back with me and we both take off our shoes. He knows how weird I get about dirtying things and such. I laugh at how well he knows me and kiss him real quick before we lay down.

I lay there, completely content with this moment and the life I have. I squeeze Kaleb's hand and roll onto my side and look at him. He looks back at me and rolls onto his side. He lets go of my hand and then rolls on top of me slightly holding himself up, as not to crush me. He gently touches his lips to mine.

I close my eyes and he kisses me again, a little less gentle, yet still soft. I open my eyes all of a sudden feeling panicked again that at any moment I'm gonna lose him, this.

I push him off me and sit up and breathe for a second. Then I grab his shirt and pull him off his back and up toward me and smash our lips together. I kiss him hard, desperately, needing his touch for some reason, as if I would never touch him again.

He, surprised at my dominance at first, goes along with it, kissing me back just as hard. He brushes his hand up and down my back. He pulls me closer. I wrap my legs around his waist. I place both my hands on his face and then brush them through his hair to the back of his head and leave them there holding our heads together.

He takes one hand off my back and slips it around my neck holding me even closer. I lower my hands down and place them on his chest gripping his shirt tightly, our lips still locked together.

I can feel his chest move up and down under my hands rapidly, his quick breaths on my face. He then moves his hand from my neck to my face caressing it. I moved away from him out of breath. He moves in and kisses me one more time softly, then pulls away still caressing my cheek.

I lean into his hand and smile. He kisses my forehead and lays back down, I lay half my body on top of his, one leg over his.

"Should I even ask?" He says and I can feel his grin through his chest.

I laugh.

"No." I say with a smile knowing he's talking about why I just attacked him with my lips.

We lay there for a while more, just together, no one else, just us, together. It's perfect, and for some reason I can't seem to shake that feeling.

After about an hour we start packing up and head back home to my house. When we get there, as usual, he gets out and hurries to my side of the car and opens the door for me. He walks me to the door of my house and kisses me goodnight.

"See you tomorrow Stel. I love you." I smile at him tired and tell him I love him too. Once inside the house I look out our window and watch him drive away.

When he's gone, I notice something different about the mood of the house, following the mood, my nose fills with a strong metallic smell.

The inside of my nostrils begin to burn from the smell. I walk into the living room and my dad is sitting on the couch blank faced, no newspaper to be seen.

I feel my body start to fill with a familiar unease as I stare at my dad who is sitting in his chair as if he were a doll, his body stiff and completely void of any emotions.

"Daddy?" My voice is shaky as I take a half step forward. My body begins to fill with terror from the lack of any response from

him let alone even acknowledgement that I was even there. I wave my arm to get his attention, still keeping my distance from him. No warning, his head whips toward me, face still expressionless he stares into my eyes. Slowly his face begins to change, his mouth moving in slow motion stretches open as if he were screaming, yet no noise comes out. His eyes locked on mine, my body shaking beneath me and I start crying terrified at the images in front of me.

I start backing up as he continues to stare at me with his terror filled silent scream, the color in his skin and hair is now fading and his image had faded into black and white and slowly, but surely not just his color, his entire being starts to fade into nothingness until he disappears into thin air right in front of me.

"No—" Tears continue to stream down my face as I lurch forward and grasp at the empty space his laughter used to fill. Now standing at the edge of the living room and kitchen I notice a movement to my right.

I whip my head toward the movement in terror and my heart starts racing at the sight in front of me. Porter's body is on the floor, no longer healthy and bright, no longer tall and happy, now small and delicate looking, the color completely drained out of him. His eyes are open, and no longer filled with life, never to see the sun again. There is red spilled all around him on the floor and on his chest, there are three large stab wounds.

I sob as a waterfall of tears fall from my face. In a jerking motion one small turn of my neck at a time I see my mom standing over him in what used to be her pink flowery apron, now a deep dark red color as blood drips from it. She's holding the knife she had used to cut vegetables in her right hand which is now also dripping with blood. She looks up at me, anger and pleasure mixing around on her face, empty of any love she had for me earlier that day.

"Surprise Stella!" She smiles at me, making me cringe. I hear the knife clatter to the ground, I look and see it lying next to my baby brother's dead body.

Judith, one slow step at a time creeps toward me, a smile still on her face. She sniffles and then wipes her nose with her hand smearing blood along the right side of her face as her expression changes from pleasure to a forced sadness. She's now only a few feet from me as she mocks my sadness and then jerks her head changing expressions again, almost as if she put on a new mask. Her mask is now of a psychotic person.

My heart is racing and I can feel a cold sweat building on my forehead as she lunges forward, grabs my shoulders, begins shaking me and yelling.

"What did you do?!
What did you do?! STELLA!"

* * *

"What did you do?!" Judith yells at me shaking me, my eyes spring open in terror. I scan the room looking for Porter. He's sitting on the floor by the far end of the couch. I jump

141

from my seat and throw my arms around him holding him desperately to my chest.

Completely ignorant of anything else going on around me I pull him away from me and begin to scan his body. No blood or new wounds, but he was also missing the happiness from the beginning of what I'm now realizing was just a dream.

I looked into his eyes, the life still there however the sun was completely gone, replaced with fear. I sigh, sad yet appreciative that he was alive right in front of me. Finally, I notice that his eyes are nervous and fluttering back and forth as if motioning to something to my left.

"Stella! What the fuck? You did NOTHING! You didn't help me prepare for my trip at all, you're such a selfish bitch."

I turn my attention away from Porter now that I know he's okay and scan the room. Judith is standing in the kitchen next to a broken beer bottle on the floor in the hallway, its metallic smell wafting through the air and into my nose. "And you're still fucking sitting there. Get the FUCK up! Clean up this mess first before you pack my shit." She rolls her eyes at me in disgust as she steps over the broken bottle and makes her way outside. *"Fucking lazy cunt…"* I hear her mumble under her breath before the door slams behind her.

I wonder if shit like that makes her feel good. Does it make her feel better about herself? I don't really feel much at all anymore when she says stuff like that, it used to sting.

It stopped a long time ago. I think of the day Porter and I will get to pack up our bags and leave here forever as I throw the last of her clothes in her bag.

My stomach knots and my chest tightens when I remember that my only plan for us to escape was taken from me this morning. Not only that, but Porter and I will probably not see Kaleb again, I doubt he'll come around again after this morning. Images of my dream begin to flash in my mind, all the blood.

Maybe that's for the better.

Smoke wafts in my face when I open the front door. My chest burns when I fight off the urge to cough. Gently, I set her bag on the picnic table. That's when I notice that Gerry's car is already here. She snatches it up, mutters something about it taking too long, throws it in the backseat of the car and then gets in the front seat. Cigarette in between her lips, she mumbles what sounds like 'see ya' and gives me a half assed wave as the car peels off.

Chapter Eleven

It's been almost a full twenty-four hours since she left and it feels unreal to be so free, to know that I don't have to be on edge as much. I can't help feeling like a weight has been lifted even just walking into the trailer.

I allow myself to walk around the house without any restrictions. I take out our clothing tub and put our dirty clothes in the basket and leave the tub out cause why not?

I drink a glass of water and leave the cup on the counter. It's like I'm allowing myself to be messy for the first time, like I can leave a glass on the counter and not be afraid of a beating later for doing so. It feels like I've been walking around with puppet wires connected to my body and moving me in the correct motions and suddenly, the wires are being cut one by one.

Snap!

I leave my makeup on the bathroom counter.

Snap!

The trash in the kitchen is full and I'm leaving it that way.

Snap!

I'm packing ONLY mine and Porter's clothes to wash.

Relief floods my entire body and I jump up and down spinning around until I fall back onto the couch behind me. I let out a long breath and then inhaled deeply through my nose and then let it out once again through my mouth.

A soft smile grows on my face while I lean my head back against the edge of the couch. I stand up feeling, what seems to be, relaxed, grab the laundry basket and head to the laundry room.

The bell at the top of the door rattles off my entrance as I open the door of the laundry room. I hear a soft bark and then quick tap, tap, taps as Sadie makes her way around the corner.

As soon as she sees me she begins to cry in excitement and begins her little butt wiggle. I appreciate the love she shares, expecting nothing in return except for maybe a pet on the head. I give her more than that of course as I bend down and wrap my arms around her neck in what I see as a hug. Her fur is soft and clean as I run my fingers through it, scratching her head a final time before I go around the corner to her owner.

"Hi Joe! I'm glad you're in here, did you just get started?"

Joe is sitting in the back corner of the room with his legs crossed and his usual smile spread from ear to ear. He chuckles when Sadie runs back to him and nudges her nose along his leg.

"I sure did kid! There's a few washers open still so it looks like you're stuck with me for a while!"

He laughs his slow hearty laugh and motions to the open washers to the left of his spinning ones. When I finish loading the clothes he pats the seat next to him.

"So, how are you sweetheart?" I'm so relaxed that I almost tell him why, I quickly remember I can't and like a knee to the chest, my breath is stolen from my lungs, the words left unsaid on the tip of my tongue.

ZIP!

A wire reattaches itself.

I'm never completely free.

"I'm doing pretty good! Porter is done with school for the summer next week, so we'll get to spend more time together!

"How have you and Sadie been, Joe?" I notice how intently he is listening, like I'm the most important person in his life right now. A soft smile filled with admiration floods his face when he looks down as Sadie snuggles up to his left leg.

"We are doing just fine. My girl and me, ya know I haven't loved anyone as much as I love my Sadie, not since my Laura girl passed a few years back anyway." My eyebrows scrunch and my head tilts in curiosity, he's never mentioned that name before. Maybe a previous dog?

"Was she a dog you had before Sadie?"

I make sure to ask this gently knowing he just said that she had passed. He chuckles and looks at me with a melancholy smile.

"No dear, Laura was my wife. She was my best friend for more than fifty years and my wife for forty of those years. You know we got married when I was only nineteen." He pauses for a moment. "It's just now dawning on me that I have never told you her name. It has taken me a long time to say her name out loud again."

He looks up as if he's recalling a precious memory which it seems as if he probably is. From the corner of my eye I can see his hands moving ever so subtly. He's been twisting his wedding ring around his finger over and over.

I fill with a tenderness for him as a single tear falls from my face. His love is so pure and unending, I can feel it flooding into me whether purposeful or not. I quickly wipe the tear from my face so that he doesn't see it.

"I can tell that you really loved her." The words come out with an unintended smile on my face. Joe just seems to bring out joy in people. He is one of the most honest and kind people I've ever encountered. I wish that I could be honest with him, that I could tell him everything and allow him to comfort me. He's not the only one I wish I could be honest with.

I want to tell Kaleb everything too. I want to have him around worry free; I want to trust him. I'm so tired of feeling trapped, I'm so tired of lying to people. Especially the kind ones.

"I really did. I'm very grateful to have Sadie though and for every time you and I get to chat!" He sends a smile my way and continues. "Sadie's pretty much all I have anymore, all of our kids moved away and live in other states and rarely ever come out here these days. Laura was the one they really loved"

He shoots me a joking smile, however I can see the sorrow behind it. My eyes widen in sadness and surprise. I honestly didn't think Joe had any kids, I would have thought they would be here frequently or that I at least would have seen them once in all the years we've been here.

It breaks my heart that the most time spent with people is in the brief and short conversations he and I have had in passing or when he's come into the office.

"Joe, would you like some company this afternoon after I finish my shift?"

I'm going to make sure that this kind and gentle man is no longer lonely, at least for the next month anyway

"I would cherish that." His body sighs with a calming smile spreading around his cheeks and eyes. My fingers begin to tingle with warmth, and I recognize the happiness I feel when I get Porter to smile, and it feels nice to do it for someone else too.

* * *

"Bye Joe! Thank you again for the tea today!" I wave toward Joe behind me as I run off toward the direction of the bus stop. It's been about a week since I started spending the afternoons and evenings with Joe before I picked Porter up from the bus stop. Today, was Porter's last day of school so he will get to spend time with Joe too. Maybe we'll even start doing dinner with him now moving forward. I smile at the thought as I make my way to Porter.

Joy surrounds me when I turn the last corner to the bus stop, I'm almost skipping, I'm enjoying myself so much. I'm almost at the spot where I usually wait for Porter when I recognize the fading white paint of Kaleb's truck across the street.

I turn toward the truck scanning for Kaleb when a car passes and momentarily blocks my view. The car passes and my eyes lock on his, he's leaning against his truck as if he was waiting for me.

I breathe in and almost instantly let go of my feelings that it might be better if he weren't around. I breathe out and hope that he wants the same thing.

I breathe in again, his face is now showing relief as he has started running toward me. Butterflies begin to flutter in my chest and I run toward him as well.

He meets me right as I'm about to jump off the sidewalk and I jumped into his arms instead.

I sigh into him as he holds me steady, gently lowering me to the ground but not releasing his grip around my waist. His face is pressed into my shoulder, and I can feel him sigh into me as well. My chest is tight and warm at the same time, I catch the tears of relief in my throat not allowing them to creep out today.

Even though I'm still filled with relief I feel my emotions mixing with guilt as well. I slowly push myself away from him.

"I'm sorry Kaleb, I didn't want to push you away, I just didn't know what else to do."

My voice breaks as I look at my feet and feel him pull me back into his arms.

"I'm sorry Stel, I'm here now. I shouldn't have let you push me away; I should have fought harder for you both." He squeezes me tighter one more time before letting me go. Right as he's letting me go the school bus pulls up loud and obnoxious.

Kids begin to run out of the bus seeming to be excited about summer break. And then I see him, excited, just not quite like the rest as he jumps out of the bus and begins to waddle over toward our normal spot that I'm not in anymore.

He looks up and sees that I'm not there and begins to scan the area and when his eyes finally lock on me, they light up and then get even brighter when he sees Kaleb next to me.

Just like I did he runs up to him and jumps off the sidewalk and into his arms. Kaleb holds him so tight and spins him around. I can feel the joy radiating off them both.

It feels almost like normal again, Kaleb taking us home. However, I know that at some point tonight, Kaleb and I will have to talk about the uncertainty floating around us.

It doesn't take long before we're pulling into the house. My heart is racing because there's a part of me that's scared Kaleb was just dropping us off and isn't going to stay and then there's this other part of me that's scared he wants to stay.

I jump out of the truck and then lift Porter out behind me. I keep glancing back and forth between Kaleb to the left of me and the path in front of me.

I feel my face heat up in embarrassment for being so nervous about what his decision will be. Kaleb shuts his door and then locks his truck. Now I have my answer so I can stop being so nervous, however that's the opposite of what my reaction is. It's almost like I have a fever. My face feels so hot.

I follow Porter's giddy little body to the front door, I quickly look back at Kaleb following behind us and send a shy smile his way before I unlock the door.

Having someone new standing in this incredibly small living space is weird and incredibly uncomfortable. He makes this space look miniature with his tall, wide frame. It seemed like he barely fit through the front door. I feel like I'm creating an awkward energy, and it seems like Porter noticed because he was looking at me like he was asking if I was okay. I gave him a light, barely noticeable nod.

He then presumed to change the entire energy in here and got super excited and pulled Kaleb to follow him to the couch. Porter's face lit up as he pulled out his puzzle from under the couch. It's almost like magic the way that Porter just completely changed everyone's mood in here as he enrolled us into putting together his puzzle with him.

Hours go by that I can just take in my complete joy in each moment, watching Porter smile and laugh and joke with Kaleb while putting together this puzzle we didn't get the chance to finish the other day.

It amazes me that Porter didn't get tired until the moment he put the last piece of the puzzle in its spot. My heart melts when Porter slumps against Kaleb almost immediately falling asleep and when Kaleb gently picks up the sleepy Porter and lays him down on the couch. Kaleb then stands up, puts a finger to his lips, and motions for me to follow him outside.

I smile and roll my eyes at the fact that he told me to be quiet, as if that isn't obvious.

The wood of the picnic table is cold against my legs when I sit across from Kaleb. Butterflies fill my chest again because I know that it's time for us to talk about all the serious stuff.

"I–" I'm at a loss for words, I'm not even sure where to start. I keep going back and forth in my mind about what to say and what would be too much. I don't know exactly what he saw the other day or what he didn't see. This could be my chance to be honest with him, but if he didn't see anything or doesn't suspect anything it could risk everything once again. He cuts me off mid overthinking.

"Stel, I'm here, you don't have to hide anymore, I know and I'm here." The sincerity in his voice brings me to my brim and I begin to overflow, overflow with anger, sadness, regret, fear.

It all rises to the surface right in front of him in a salty, snotty, wet mess that he pays no mind to, he comes to my side and pulls me into his chest anyway.

I allow him to hold me for who knows how long. All I know for sure is that this is the first time I can remember in a very long time that I've allowed myself to completely let go and allow someone else to take over, if only for a moment.

It feels like it's been forever that I've been held in his embrace. I feel safer right now in this moment than I have in a very, very long time.

Gently I push myself away from him and I let go once more, only this time with words. It's like vomit flowing out of me and floating into the air.

I tell him.

I tell him everything and he listens so intently.

For the first time it feels like I'm allowing someone to really see me. It seems like it's been forever when I finally take a breath and stop talking. I look up at him from my shaky hands nervously waiting for his response. He looks down at his hands and then back up at me.

"I'm so sorry Stel, I never would have thought that Judith could be like this. Do you want me to take you somewhere you can talk to someone?" I can feel my eyebrows instantly pull together.

"Wh-what do you mean?" Now he is looking at me with scrunched eyebrows.

"You know so you can tell someone what's going on and you all can get the help you ne–"

"NO!" I don't even let him finish his sentence. I can feel the anger building inside of me, it's like he didn't listen to anything I said. "Did you not hear anything I said?"

"I did bu–"

"No, no, no, I can't tell anyone, don't you see that? They'll separate us, you *know* that!"

I'm now on my feet pacing back and forth, I can feel the tangles I'm creating in my hair from rubbing it around on my head.

"Stel, I'm just trying to help, you're obviously too close to this to see what's best!" He slightly raises his voice and now I'm pissed, where the fuck has he been to know what's best?! I stop my pacing and slowly turn my body toward him.

"Excuse me? The fuck would you know about what's best for me and *my* little brother. You barely fucking know us Kaleb, you pop up out of nowhere and try and be the fucking hero? No, it really is on me, huh, I don't know why I felt any other way, it's always been this way. You left, just like *him,* I never should have trusted that you would understand. That ten year old boy in there?"

I swing my hand up pointing toward the trailer. "That you say you want to help? *I raised him!*" I spit the last part at him, how dare he?

"You know NOTHING! You have no idea what I've been through, you have no idea the responsibilities I've had to take on!"

My mind is screaming, I feel like I can't breathe, I need to calm down, he can't leave here mad, what if he tells someone?

"No one will believe you, you know?"

"What?" He finally cuts in. "Stel stop, I'm only trying to help, I would never tell anyone, however I think *you should.*

She could really, *really* hurt you two." He says this gently and steps a little closer. "She already has, hasn't she?" He says this and reaches his hand toward my face where my scar lay. I slap his hand away and take two big steps back.

"I know how to manage her now. I don't need your protection Kaleb, I just need to find a way to get custody of Porter, now with no money. I'll figure it out. I always do. I only have a few months before I'm eighteen, I'll figure this out." I say this and start pacing back and forth in front of him. "Look if you can't support me in finding another way, then you need to go and you should go ahead and forget about us when you do."

"Stel – I won't allow her to continue to add marks on you."

"Leave it alone. You don't have to stick around, Kaleb. Just go." He stands there a mix of anger and sadness spreads across his face. "Kaleb GO!" I yell the last part and it seems to shake him awake a little because he's now slowly backing up and climbing into his truck. I stand outside and watch him drive away quickly brushing away the single tear I couldn't hold back.

I feel the loneliness creep right back in with the cold breeze that passes by and chills my bones. I cross my arms and.

ZIP!

Another puppet wire puts itself back into place.

The wires walk me back inside and start cleaning up the little messes I let be earlier when I thought I was free.

Chapter Twelve

S mack! I slap the table in front of me where the lowest face card just lay and let out a small giggle at the shock on Porter's face and the disbelief on Joe's as he shakes his head and begins to laugh along with me.

I feel constant here, like my body is finally steadying itself, like the breath I just took in won't be the last when I let it out. My one foot planted on the wooden porch under me and my other one tucked between my thigh and the plastic lawn chair holding me upright.

Porter pushes the cards toward me with a very forced grumpy look on his face. At that I fill the porch with the sound of my own laughter.

I feel like I could stay here forever, another moment I wish I could live the rest of my life in. So, I lean back and take in the overwhelmingly wonderful picture in front of me.

Porter to my left leaning back almost too far in the plastic chair, his chubby little cheeks scrunched up into his eyes, head tilted backward allowing his curly blonde hair to fall out of his face all while he's letting a boisterous laugh escape from his lips, unreluctantly.

To my right is Joe, whom I've only ever seen give me soft, gentle and caring smiles, is now bent forward, slapping his knee, his eyes squeezed shut from the heavy smile spread across his face as he lets out his own booming cackle. I allow myself to welcome this moment and take the picture with my mind.

Who knew my own laughter could create such beauty.

Porter leans forward and notices that I'm not laughing anymore and lets out a little giggle.

"Why so serioussss Stelly?" He says dragging on his words and then sticks his fingers in his mouth to pull on his cheeks with his fingers, crossing his eyes and then starts shaking his head back and forth making fun of me.

I jump out of my seat and lunge toward him, reaching my arms out tickling him as he starts squirming in his chair laughing and laughing.

The air around me thickens with warmth not necessarily because of the actual temperature outside, but because of the warmth in this moment. Laughter and love spreading through the air like the wind, I look around and it's almost as if I'm looking through rose colored glasses. My heart swells up inside me and in that moment, I remove any constrictions toward letting myself feel the happiness around me. It's not dangerous here to show joy.

I'm safe for now.

Porter and I help Joe clean up outside before we make our way to the other side of Joe's trailer to head home. I look up toward our trailer and there is now a truck parked outside. Kaleb's truck. Just like when he was at the bus stop, he's leaning up against the bed, waiting for us to get home. This time, however, he's standing there with flowers in one hand and grocery bags in the other.

I kept my same pace when walking toward him this time, however Porter did not. Before I knew it Kaleb was picking Porter up and swinging him around and giving him a big hug. When Kaleb finally puts Porter down, he gasps in excitement looking inside the plastic bags and then looks up to Kaleb.

"Is that cereal??" Kaleb just laughs and nods. Porter then pauses and looks down at his feet nervously. "Can I have some?" He then looks up with a cautious pouty look on his face.

"What?? Of course! This is for you bud! You can have all of it!" Porter immediately goes back to being excited and starts jumping up and down.

I finally make my way over to the two of them. I'm not exactly sure what to expect, I'm just hoping he remembers me saying not to come back, unless he can keep his mouth shut.

"Hi Kaleb." I send a cautious smile his way. My hands are crossed behind my back and my nails are digging into my hands nervously.

I really don't want to be disappointed again. I look down at my feet and then back up at him. "Thank you for the groceries."

"Oh these?" He lifts the bags up slightly. "Yeahhh, I just told Porter they were for you guys because he got so excited and then I felt bad." He shrugs looking away nonchalantly and I can feel my cheeks instantly get hot in embarrassment.

"I–sorry I shouldn't have assumed." He turns his face back toward me and is now smiling like he's holding back a laugh.

"Stel, I'm kidding, it's my pleasure. It's obvious to me now though that we need to talk about a few things before we can just go right back to having fun."

Duh… I still don't know whether or not we're on the same page about Porter and my situation. I give him a look that hopefully says *obviously.*

"Porter!" He comes running over here from the picnic table and then smiles at me. I giggle at his goofiness and then ask him through my laugh if he could put the groceries away.

He just starts nodding before he takes the grocery bags from Kaleb and then runs them inside. As soon as Porter is no longer in ear shot, Kaleb takes a step closer to me so we're only about a foot away from each other. It takes everything in me to not take a step backward.

"Look Stel." He reaches toward me resting his hand on my shoulder for a moment and once again it takes focus to not pull away from him.

"I could never forget about you, either of you. I mean, Stel a big part of why I came back here was in hopes of seeing you again." He sighs and brings his hand back to himself. "I– I won't say anything. I won't push you to say anything, we've just gotta come up with a different plan for the two of you."

It's crazy to me yet the idea of having someone to help me brainstorm another way out of here lights me up. It's like once again I'm not alone anymore.

"Deal." I say it so quickly and my attitude has obviously changed.

Kaleb is just looking at me with his eyebrows raised as if to say, 'really?'.

I laugh, nod and then start to walk past him, but grab his hand at the last second and pull him behind me into the trailer.

* * *

Something about this last week has just felt different. Having Kaleb here all day almost every day has completely changed the way the trailer feels, it's like when he's here it almost feels like a home. Every day he comes back in the morning, makes us breakfast, and will then spend the rest of the day with us either going over to Joe's and playing cards or going to the pond with us or even listening to me read with Porter. He even hangs out with Porter while I'm working or they'll both come spend time with me in the office.

Every night after Porter goes to sleep Kaleb and I will sneak outside and talk for hours. Just like tonight, I feel my knee brush against the cold jagged wood of the picnic table.

Kaleb is sitting across from me with his hands folded in front of him on the table. My hands are also on the table only inches from his. I can feel a wave of heat coming from him and I have the urge to reach my hand just a little closer and wrap his hands in mine. Except, I don't. I just leave my hands close enough to feel the tension, just not quite touching him.

"Kaleb?" He looks to me ready to listen to anything. His expression is so gentle and comforting, it makes me feel like I could tell him anything. I want to just talk to him, tell him all the things that have been wreaking havoc in my mind, but I feel guilty even thinking about them. "What if I don't want to be a mom anymore? What if I just want to be his sister." I trail off and look away, guilt flooding my entire body as soon as the words escape my lips.

"Stel…" His voice is so soft and understanding, just enough to make me look back toward him. He smiles at me tenderly. "You have no reason to feel guilty for that. You're not his mom, you are his sister. You didn't choose this life for yourself, and still you've done an incredible job raising that kid."

I allow a single tear to creep down my cheek. I didn't realize until just then how much weight was lifted from me just by saying that out loud.

I feel so good when I'm with Kaleb, like I can finally just be Stella and not a protector or a mom or anything, just myself.

We sit like that for a little longer and I allow myself to feel safe. I can feel the moonlight on my skin. The calm white light is cool and somehow gives off a comforting yet eerie experience to the night.

The moonlight rests on Kaleb's face in all the perfect places accentuating all his best features. The soft arch of his nose, the fullness of his pouty lips and the bright green of his eyes.

He glances up at me and I realize that I've been staring at him. I quickly turn away, my face rapidly heating up. I feel like I hear him chuckle, but I'm so in my head I can't really tell.

"So, I told my dad that I found you." I snap my head back toward him and he quickly understands my response. "Don't worry, I didn't mention anything about Judith, just that we were spending time together and how much I like Porter."

He reaches across the table and grabs my hand as if to reassure me when he says this. I wonder what he said to his dad, I'm sure he asked about more than just me and Porter, he had to have asked questions about Judith and *my dad*.

That's it!

I jump up from the table in excitement.

"Kaleb you're a genius!" He looks at me confused. "That's the plan!" His body shifts upright when he realizes what I'm talking about.

"Wait, hold on a second Stel, my dad is in no place to be a caretaker right now, that's far from a good option, I'm not sure that the courts wou–"

"No, no." I say shaking my head. "*My* dad Kaleb! My dad! All we have to do is find him! I'm sure that if he found out what he left us with he would take us in."

I'm now pacing back and forth in front of him. I can't believe I hadn't thought of this before.

"Kaleb we have to find him, you'll help us right?" I look at him desperate for him to say yes. He's now grinning along with me and my excitement.

"Of course I will." He pulls his hair out of his face and smiles up at me again. "Stel this could actually work."

I run over to him and wrap my arms around him practically jumping into his lap.

He's right, this could actually work.

Chapter Thirteen

I woke up this morning full of doubt. What if we don't find him? Or worse, what if he doesn't care?

I move mindlessly through the morning stuck in a loop of questioning this idea. It's not until Kaleb shows up with coffee, breakfast and a notebook that the loop stops.

"A notebook?" I tilt my head to the side when I point at the black wire bound book in his hand.

"How else are we gonna keep track of any hints we get as to where John is?" He smiles at me completely free of any doubt and if he had any he wasn't showing it.

"So, you're sure about this idea?" I look down and pick at my nails for a moment before I hear him sigh.

"Stel, what happened last night? You were so excited." He walks over to me and pulls my chin up to look at him. "Huh?" He pushes me a little further to answer.

"I just–What if he doesn't give a shit? I mean he *chose* to leave, don't you think if he wanted us he would have come looking by now?"

I feel a pang in my chest when I say the words because they sound even more probable when I actually speak them aloud.

"Yes, he left, but you have no idea what he could be thinking right now, maybe he misses you guys, and he's is too afraid to face you? He could even think that you're better off without him. Not having any idea what the reality even is. My point is Stel is that there's a million things he could be thinking and the only way to know which one it is, is to go find out."

I nod my head, what he's saying does make sense and it's true I have no idea what he's thinking, I barely even remember what he looks like anymore.

"Plus, what other choice do we have Stel?" He says this part a little quieter. Again, he's got a point, we're doing this because it's our last option.

"You're right, so what do we do first?" I say, ready to get started. He smiles at my seriousness all of a sudden and then reaches behind him briefly and then turns back to me holding up two paper bags.

"Breakfast."

Kaleb amazes me the way he can always sweeten any situation. It seems to be good for Porter having him around.

We're always having fun when he's here, it might also be because Judith hasn't been here, even so, I choose to believe that Kaleb brings a lot of joy to us.

Judith or no Judith.

We finish breakfast and I pretty quickly go back to my original question.

"Where do we start?" Kaleb laughs and gives in to my tenacity. "So, I was thinking that we look through Judith's bedroom first, I'll do that so that I can make sure everything goes back to the way it was. Could you call your dad and get any info from him you can?"

Kaleb nods and then Porter looks at me like he's saying, well what about me? I giggle and motion for him to follow me into the trailer.

"Just be very careful where and how you move things, bud." I say this anyway even though he already knows.

Porter and I each take a side of the small room with barely enough room to walk on each side of the bed. I start by looking in the cupboards on the side of the bed and then the cupboards above the bed. There's nothing, just her shitty clothes, some food wrappers, empty cigarette boxes and a few beer bottles.

I check underneath the bed and again, nothing. So, I lift the mattress and under the mattress is a flat piece of plywood. Toward the end of the frame there's a hole in the plywood. I lift the mattress as high as I can.

"Porter, come here!" I hear his quick movements and then I motion toward the hole with my head. "Pull that open." He nods almost giddy.

I can tell that this just feels like a mystery game to him. He was only three months old when dad left so he really has no emotional connection to him.

When he lifts it up there's a beaten up, tattered shoe box underneath in a space just barely wide enough and tall enough for it. You can see indents on the top of the shoe box from where the wood squished it down time and time again.

Both Porter and I get excited at the sight of the box. It could be a clue, something to lead us to him. Porter grabs the box and I quickly put the mattress down so we can look through the box.

"Kaleb! We found something!" I shout through the door as Porter places the shoe box on the living room floor. I look at Porter, my fingers grasping at the lid and he nods, giving me the go-ahead.

Kaleb comes rushing in just in time to see the lid fall to the floor. Porter and I both lean over the box, eager to see what's inside.

On top is an old black and silver men's seiko watch. I pull that out first and when I do a memory flashes in my mind. My small hand holding my dad's larger one with this watch attached to it. I'm sure of it.

"This was his." I stay focused on the box, not even looking up to say this. Under the watch was what looked like some old, faded receipts and some random scraps of paper. I lift those out of the box and underneath is a silver flip phone. I snap it open right away and hold down the power button. No luck.

"Looks like we'll have to get a charger for it. No biggie." Kaleb saw the disappointment on my face and responded with this to try and get ahead of it.

I nod reluctantly and keep digging through the box, there's a few receipts in here for a phone bill, which my guess is that it's for this phone, so it's probably just Judith's spare phone anyway.

I show the receipts to Kaleb and it seems like he has the same thought because his face also drops a little.

"What? I don't get it." Porter says looking back and forth between the two of us.

"Nothin bud, we just think that this might be a spare phone for Judith."

"Why would she have that?" His face is scrunched in confusion. My guess was that it was for different hookups, however I don't want to tell him that.

"My best guess would be that maybe this was an old work phone for her and she's still paying the bills as an extra emergency phone?" I shrug my shoulders when I say that.

"I guueeesss that makes sense." He still looks puzzled for a moment. He brushes it off and focuses back on the box.

I pull out the last of the receipts and on the very bottom of the box is a picture of all of us from ten years ago. By all of us I mean Paul, Cora and Kaleb too. Pain rushes through me at the sight of all our smiling faces. Judith looks like a normal human being gripping tight to a baby she actually looks to care about in the photo. And then there's me gripping tightly to my dad's hand, an obvious daddy's girl.

"Is that us?" Porter looks amazed as he points to the photo.

"Yeah bud, it is." I fight back tears, it's been ten years since I've seen my father's face and yet the image of him that I had in my head was still fairly accurate. I don't quite understand why it's so hard to look at him, it's like the picture of him smiling so sincerely is building a weird mix of anger and yearning to see the smile in person again.

"I didn't know he had blonde hair like me! Stelly you look a lot like him!" His words send a pang to my stomach.

"I do, don't I?" I force a smile trying hard not to show the turmoil going on in my head.

"You both have an interesting mix of the both of them, however you both have more of John's features than Judith's. What I think is the coolest part, is that the two of you look more alike than you look like either of them." I look up to

Kaleb and smile sincerely, he couldn't have said anything better.

"Is that you Kaleb??" Porter gets really excited after finally noticing this. "And is that your mom??" I wince knowing that answering that might be painful for him and when I look to check his expression, I can tell that I'm right. It's just barely noticeable, however there is a spark of pain behind his eyes. "She's really pretty, you look a lot like her, Kaleb."

Porter is so kind and innocent and I can see how hard Kaleb is forcing himself to hide his own pain the same way I was.

"She really is beautiful isn't she, bud?" I say this and gently take the photo from his hand and place it back into the box. "I think we should move on to something else maybe. Kaleb, did you talk with your dad?"

I listen for a response as I pack the items back into the box. When he doesn't say anything, I look up at him and he has a look on his face like he forgot about something really important, like he forgot something in the oven.

"Kaleb, what? What happened?" I can feel myself starting to panic slightly.

"I can't believe I forgot about my conversation with him! I got so caught up in the box you found, anyway that doesn't matter, he said he doesn't have his phone number anymore, he lost it a while back switching phones and just never wrote it down." He starts pacing and rambling a little. "But Stel, I got an address."

My eyes widen looking at him. It's hard to hold back my hope at the thought, we might have a clue.

This might be possible.

"Stel, he mentioned something else." The way his voice drops worries me. "He said that when your dad left, it was like he just disappeared with barely any contact to my dad or John's parents. He says when he stopped contacting him, Judith seemed to have a lot of information, stuff that John never told him until a few days after over text or email. Either way he said that she would probably know the most."

I appreciate him for filling me in on all the details, however Judith is a dead end, so she doesn't matter right now.

I nod and then move on.

"What's the address?"

Chapter Fourteen

On the way there, Kaleb explained that it was the address of where John was working before he left and that Paul said he couldn't promise that it was the same business anymore.

He also told us that ten years ago it was a newspaper, John was apparently working his way up to journalist and that the newspaper was still around, he just wasn't sure if they were at the same location.

I made sure to bring the picture we found, so that I could show people what he looked like when asking about him. I also brought the cell phone just in case so that we could get a charger for it. It was worth a shot to at least see what was on it.

The drive felt a lot longer than it was, it was like every second ticked by twice as long. My mind keeps doubting any kind of success in this mission. I know I should keep more positive; I just can't shake this feeling that maybe this isn't the best option.

"Shit!"

"What?" Kaleb instantly sounds worried.

"I completely forgot to tell Sarah that I was going to be gone."

I pull out my phone and quickly dial her number. She answers in her joyful tone, just as always.

I explain to her that I had to leave suddenly due to a family emergency. She sounds worried and tells me not to worry about it, that she'll have the office covered for the rest of the week and just to tell her when I'm ready to come back.

I sigh in relief and then I realize that Kaleb has been with us almost all day every day this summer.

"Kaleb, what about your job?" I look at him concerned, he chuckles before he responds.

"I talked with my uncle at the beginning of the summer and told him that a friend of mine needed my help this summer and he filled my spot with a part time summer apprentice." It always surprises me how prepared he is. I feel the truck begin to slow.

"We're here!" Kaleb practically shouts as he throws the truck in park and then looks at both Porter and me with an excited smile spread across his face.

I stare at him nervously and like always he softens his smile for me. He gets out of the truck and comes to my side opening the door and then motioning for me to follow him. I help Porter down and we follow Kaleb inside.

Relief floods my body when I see the writing on the door. It's still a newspaper company. My pace quickens as I begin to lead us through the front door.

"Excuse me." I wave at the petite woman behind the front desk. She looks at me slightly annoyed, probably because a bunch of kids just walked in here.

"Do you by any chance know if someone still works here that worked here ten years ago?" She smacks her lips looking up at me, her blowout bouncing every time she chews on her gum.

"Yeah, why?" She keeps staring at me like she's just irritated that I'm here, and yet I could care less because someone still works here that used to work with him.

"My dad used to work here about ten years ago and I was hoping to speak to anyone who may have known him." The secretary rolls her eyes, picks up her phone and punches in a few numbers.

"Hi Mary, yeah there's three kids here who want to talk to you." She's nodding her head while listening to Mary on the other line. She "mmhmm's" one more time and then hangs up the phone. "Yup she's busy, sorry, you can schedule an appointment if you'd like." She sends me a fake smile.

"Please–Please ask her again, please tell her I'm John Peterson's daughter, maybe she'll remember his name." Her eyes light up when I say this and she takes no more convincing before she's picking up the phone and dialing the same numbers again.

"Mary, John Peterson's daughter is here to see you." She responds with a few more "mmm's" until she hangs up the phone again, this time she is now ushering us down a hallway and into an office. I look at both Kaleb and Porter with confusion very obviously spread across my face.

Behind the desk in the office is an older woman with short grey hair and big round glasses resting on the bridge of her nose. She smiles brightly as soon as she sees us.

"You must be Stella." She says as she walks around the desk, taking my hands in her own. "You were about *this* big the last time I saw you." She motions to a height just below her waist.

"You've met me?" I can feel the surprise on my face.

"Of course sweetheart!" She smiles gently before returning behind her desk. "Your daddy used to bring you in here all the time." She quickly turns from me to Porter. "And you must be Porter." He nods a few times, and she laughs at his silence. "You were just barely born the last time I saw you, my how you both have grown so much!"

"Pardon me if this is rude, it's just—why do you remember us so well?" I shake my head because I truly don't understand, I mean it's been ten years.

"Well darlin, your daddy was the point of gossip for a few years around here after he disappeared."

"Why do you say disappeared?" I interrupt her because this is the second time we've heard that now.

"I say disappeared because he did darlin', at least around here he did. One day he was here workin' hard and building his way up to being a full-time journalist and then the next he just stopped showing up. A day or two after he stopped showing up, we got an email saying he wouldn't be coming back, that he needed a fresh start somewhere else. This surprised everyone in the office because of how fast he was building his career here, to the point that we thought about filing a missing person report, except your mama always told us that he just up and walked out on ya'll. We didn't feel like we actually had any reason to call anymore."

I couldn't hold back the shock that he was so popular around here because he deserted his family.

"So, why did y'all come here today missy, hmm?" She leans her plump frame back in her chair, folding her hands in her lap.

"I'm trying to find my dad, when he left here, he left me too and I just really need to find him. I was hoping you might know something?" I can feel my face pleading with her. She squints her eyes at me for a moment, looks out her door to see if anyone is around and then leans in looking back and forth between the three of us.

"Now, I'm not technically allowed to give out current or previous employees information, however if you promise not to tell anyone, I think I can help y'all out." She winks at me and then leans back again and begins typing into the big white bulky box on her desk.

A few more minutes of typing and then she pulls out a piece of paper and begins writing. My nerves are high right now, hoping that whatever information she gives us is actually helpful.

"Alright my girl, here is the phone number that we had on file and when we got the email about him not coming back, he also sent a change of address form to us for any checks etc. I wrote that down as well." She smiles brightly at me and hands me the paper. She then leans over as if she wanted us to lean in as well, so I did. "Now, normally we don't keep stuff on record this long, but I kept his stuff saved just in case. So, keep this between us." I can tell she's done because she's leaned back in her chair again.

"Thank you so much, Mary." I look down at the paper and feel a wave of relief and excitement wash over me at the sight of the address and phone number. It didn't even matter to me that the address was a little over a four-hour drive from us.

As we are walking out the door, Mary waves at us to stop.

"There's also one more place you might want to check out." She says this in a loud whisper. "A few blocks from here there is a rock-climbing gym, you might want to check it out! There might still be a few people over there that were climbing back when John was!"

I thanked her again profusely, and we made our way out of the office and back into the truck.

I pull out my phone immediately and dial the phone number. As soon as I hit call a pit falls into my stomach and I can feel myself become instantly nervous. Any idea I might have had of what to say instantly disappears.

What am I supposed to say? 'Hey, pops, I know you completely abandoned us, but could you come to save us now?'

The phone rings once and then goes straight to voicemail. It's his voice. I didn't necessarily remember it before this, yet I recognized it instantly. Not live, but it's his phone number for sure. His voice even sounds the same. Happy and calm all at once. Always able to light up a room with ease.

The voicemail beeps to start the recording and I immediately hang up the phone.

"So?" Kaleb nudges me. "What happened?"

"Isn't it obvious? It went to voicemail." I roll my eyes at him frustrated.

"Why didn't you leave a message?"

"Are you serious?" Leave a message? Hell no. "That's not really the kind of thing you leave over voicemail, I'd rather talk to him. I'll try him again tomorrow."

"What about the rock climbing place?" Porter's voice chimes into the conversation now, excited to be a part of our adventure.

"That's a really good idea, what do you think?" Kaleb looks at me with his eyebrows raised. I nod and he starts down the road until we come across the building that has to be it.

Kaleb parks and when I look more closely at it, it's definitely the right place.

I jump out of the truck, wasting no time.

As I push open the door, greeting the woman at the front desk,"Hi, I was wondering if there's anyone here today who's been coming here for ten years or longer?" The girl at the front desk seems to be startled almost by my bluntness, she quickly recovers her ponytail swinging as she shakes her head and then smiles at me.

"You know Charlie might actually be here today, he's been coming here regularly for fifteen years. Why do you ask sweety?" She tilts her head in helpful curiosity. I quickly pull out the picture and show it to her.

"We're looking for this man and we're hoping that someone here might know something or have a way to contact him." I feel my shoulders drop when she begins to shake her head and then she perks up real quick like she just had an idea.

"Let me go see if I can find Charlie, I'll ask him if he's willing to talk to you guys, okay?" She smiles brightly again before she turns and runs off to the opposite side of the gym and out of our view.

I turn around and just like I figured they would be, Porter and Kaleb are right on my heels. As soon as we got here I was busting through the doors of the gym not waiting for either of them.

I look up at Kaleb, filled with impatience. He looks at me and can tell right away that my mind is anything but relaxed. He reaches his hand up and rests it gently on my shoulder rubbing it slightly. It doesn't take long after this, that Porter notices as well. At first he just looks up at me apprehensively and then as if something shifts in him he runs to me and wraps his tiny arms around my waist.

"It's okay Stelly, we'll figure this out." I know what he meant, and it wasn't just finding John either. He was talking about *everything*. I'll never stop being amazed at how empathetic he is.

A voice clears behind us, and I jump slightly before turning around. A tall man with greys growing throughout his beard stands behind us with his hands behind his back. His build is tall and stocky. His back straight and head high, his presence felt very regal. Yet when you looked into his eyes it was instant comfort with a welcoming smile that was spreading warmth through the whole room.

"Good morning!" His voice boomed from his chest and yet somehow still came out gentle. "I'm Charlie" He reaches his hand out and one by one he greets each one of us personally. As if to show him respect he shakes Kaleb's hand with a strong steady grip. He grabs my hand gently and wraps his other over the top and with Porter he shakes his hand vigorously up and down until they are both laughing at the goofy handshake.

"Rachel tells me that you are looking for someone and that I may be of some help." He nods his head and waves his hand, signaling to us that he's ready for information. I clear my throat and feel almost nervous, not out of fear, more of a nervousness where I want to make sure this man respects me.

"Thank you for being willing to help us. This is who we are looking for his name is John and this picture is probably about ten years old and he probably looks quite a bit older now. I barely recognized him when I saw this picture, that's mostly because it had been so long since I'd seen what he looked like and somehow when I saw this picture I recognized him instantly and–" Kaleb gently touches my arm and I realize a little too late how many words had just come out of my mouth. "Sorry." I look down at my feet.

"It's quite alright dear, I tend to have that effect on people for some reason. People just seem to be comfortable opening up to me." He smiles down at me and quickly pats my shoulder. "As far as this picture goes, by any chance is your name Stella?" My eyes widened and I stand there frozen not knowing what to say. Charlie chuckles at my reaction and I want to giggle along with him, and yet I can't seem to push myself toward that reaction. The only emotion swimming around in my head at this moment is melancholy.

If so many people remember me and dad we couldn't have left anything, other than a good memory behind for these people. It hurts to know that at one point we were the kind of family that people remembered for good reasons. I feel myself disengaging and the muffled noises of what sounded like a conversation.

Before I can stop it I can feel my chest burning and anger building inside of me, anger I can't seem to control. I'm about to snap at them when the sound of Porter's giggle snaps me out of my emotional turmoil. I allow myself to focus back in on the conversation and realize that Porter is giggling at Charlie reminiscing about me when I was younger. Apparently when I would come in with John I would run around the gym like a wild child and every time we got here, one of the first things I would do was go find Charlie.

I feel embarrassment creep up for a moment until I force myself to join in on the laughter. Sometimes I feel like if I fake certain emotions, then maybe someday I'll actually feel them. I shake my head a little realizing that we were getting off track.

"Charlie," I cut in attempting to redirect the conversation "It's apparent that you recognize our dad, do you have any idea where he went? Or maybe a way to contact him?" Charlie's face instantly sinks.

"Unfortunately, I do not. He was coming in regularly one minute and then without notice or anything we just never saw him again."

He looks down at his hand, sadness spreading throughout his face. "John and I used to climb together at least three times a week for probably a year and then when he left I was fairly worried until we heard through the grapevine that he left you and your mom all alone. I was disappointed in my friend for leaving you all and hurt that he didn't speak to me at all about what was going on with him. He just disappeared and we moved on." He shrugs and looks at me with apologetic eyes.

My shoulders drop in disappointment, another day wasted. We can't keep wasting time when we only have so little for a plan that may not even work.

"Hey!" Charlie perks up and looks between the three of us with excitement. "How about for old times sake, I give all three of you a climbing lesson?"

He places his hands on his hips and I can feel the weight of the room lifting. All I want to do is leave and start on the next thing to find dad and then I look at Porter and he's jumping up and down in excitement. I can't tell him no.

"Alright, that sounds pretty great." I smile and I can feel myself growing excited the more I surrender to the idea of having some fun today.

It doesn't take long for Charlie to get the three of us set up in climbing gear. Charlie focuses on Porter first which I sincerely appreciate. I step back standing next to Kaleb and watch Porter's face change from focused on what Charlie is saying to giggling.

"I love seeing him light up like this." Kaleb is smiling at the sight of Porter and Charlie, the same as I was.

"Me too." I smile and soak up this feeling. It feels magical. I lean toward Kaleb and bump him with my hip. He looks down at me and wraps his arm around me squeezing me tight to his side before he drops his arm back down to his side.

"Porter deserves to be a kid. I'm gonna do everything in my power to make sure he gets that Stel. I care about you both so much." My face instantly heats up at his words. Something in my stomach churns almost like a stomachache but a good stomach ache. Is this what people refer to as butterflies? If so, I do not like them.

I look up at Kaleb and my chest warms at the sight of him. His dirty blonde almost brown, curly hair flops around his head when he moves. There's something about the curve of his nose and the pout of his lips that always makes me want to be closer to him.

His green eyes meet mine, catching me staring at him. I blush again and look down at my feet. I can feel the smile growing on his face without even looking at him.

"Thank you, Kaleb. I don't know how we could have done any of this without you. You've changed our lives in so many ways. You have no idea how grateful I am to you." I can feel a tear fighting to push its way down my cheek as I blink it away. I quickly look up to Kaleb, stand up on my tippy toes and pull his cheek to my lips. I push him away and then run over to Porter.

When I get to him, he's jumping up and down in excitement and Charlie is prepping him to scale the wall in front of us. It doesn't take long before I'm watching Porter's small body quickly move farther from the ground like it's the easiest thing he's ever done.

He reaches up for the next hold when his right foot slips and he's falling before I can even blink.

I gasp and run forward scared he was going to get hurt, however Charlie moved into action before I could even get to him.

With his left foot forward, Charlie pulled the rope tight and Porter stopped midair. His little body was bouncing up and down and I realized that he was giggling uncontrollably.

It appeared from here that he was feeling something, however it's something I don't know that I've ever felt before.

Pure joy.

Chapter Fifteen

We now have about a week and a half until Judith comes back. We don't have any more time to waste. I feel anxiety building within me.

My feet moving across the gravel beneath me robotically taking me back and forth, back and forth. My body moves in line with the side of the trailer as I pace, impatience filling me.

I stare at my packed bags sitting on the picnic table waiting for Porter's bags to join them. I can't take it anymore.

I swing the front door open and look inside to try and see what they were doing. Porter is getting up off the couch while Kaleb throws his pillowcase of clothes and bathroom products over his shoulder.

"Finally!" I sigh in relief as they both move toward me. I hold the door open for them and then quickly lock it behind them.

As soon as Porter makes it close to the truck, I begin ushering him into it and pick him up putting him inside. I rush the process and then jump in myself.

We have a long drive to Seattle with no idea what we're even going to find or if it's going to be a waste of time. I wanted to leave by eight so that we could get to the house by early afternoon except this morning's process took much longer than I thought it would. It's now nine thirty and we're just now getting into the truck. We're about an hour and half later than I wanted.

I clench my fists, slightly digging my nails into my palms. I fight the urge to snap at these two for being late and push my frustration aside. We're still going to get there before evening.

"Alright!" Kaleb jumps into the truck smiling and excited like we weren't an hour and a half behind. His lack of awareness pokes a nerves, and I can't hold back my scoff and eye roll.

I regret this instantly because Kaleb is now staring at me, eyes narrowed. "Nope, that's not how we're going to start this four-hour drive." Kaleb shrugs and jumps back out of the truck. He comes over to the passenger side ripping the door open and reaches over me unbuckling my seatbelt.

"No, no, no, no! Kaleb!" I shout as he reaches down, pulling me out of the truck and throwing me over his shoulder. I squirm in his arms yelling at him to put me down until he sets me down on top of the picnic table. "What the fuck." I glare at him, arms crossed.

"Stel, I know we're running behind and I also know you don't want to be irritated this whole trip, right? So, take a breath and we'll get there when we get there." He smiles attempting to create understanding. I roll my eyes again. "Okay that's it, if reason isn't working then I'll just have to go with force."

"Wha–" Before I can say anything more, he's stepped closer to me and is now tickling me. I can't control the laughter that comes with it. "Sto-" Laughter. I can't help myself and the irritation slowly begins to fade away. Kaleb can tell and he stops taking a step back, I smile at him and he laughs.

"Better?" He puts his hands on his hips like he just completed a long and arduous task that he was very proud of.

"Yes" I can hear the smile in my own voice. We both get back into the truck and I can feel the difference in the energy in here instantly.

"You're right this is much better." Kaleb pushes me playfully from the other side of the truck. I can hear a faint giggle come from Porter when he does this.

"Ohhhh you think it's funny huh?" I smile devilishly and begin tickling Porter and the space is instantly filled with joy. Kaleb was right, this is much better. I make sure Porter is buckled and then I buckle myself. My back rests gently against the soft seat of the truck. I lean into it and allow a smile to grow on my face. Not for any particular reason, just because. I'm learning to really appreciate a 'just because' smile.

* * *

The four hours fly by and before I know it, we're parked outside of an old blue house with dirty white trim. My hand begins to shake as I lift up the sheet of paper with the address on it. I check again just to make sure that the numbers and street match. Sure enough, they match perfectly.

"Okay, let's do this." My body feels like jelly when I jump out of the truck, I can't tell yet if it's because we've been in the car or if it was the nerves.

Porter follows right behind me seemingly unphased by the situation, in fact he seems more excited. Possibly because for him this probably feels more like an adventure than something dire, the way it feels for me.

Kaleb also follows behind me. I shake out my arms and take a deep breath attempting to calm myself down. My steps become more and more confident the closer I get to the dirt-stained front door. Before I know it I'm standing at the doorstep.

I look behind me for some reassurance, both Kaleb and Porter nod giving it to me without any question. Slowly my hand rises and I knock on the door.

I wait for a response for about thirty seconds before I look back at Porter and Kaleb again. Kaleb shrugs and Porter just looks puzzled. I knock again and wait. This time I hear slow shuffling to the door and then a raspy voice yells at us.

"No solicitors!" I'm taken aback by the sound of her voice. I wasn't expecting a female voice, let alone an older one.

"I'm sorry, ma'am, we're not soliciting. Would you mind–" Bang! It sounds like she smacked the door.

"I said, NO solicitors!" Before I can say anything else I hear the sound of her shuffling away from the door. It doesn't seem like she'd come back to the door even if I knocked again.

I turn away and start walking back to the truck. Before I cross the street, I look back at the house one more time to see if there's any kind of a clue or something from the outside that could maybe lead us to Dad.

That's when I see it.

The mail slot in her front door. That's it. I motion for Kaleb and Porter to hurry up. I quickly explain to them my idea to make a copy of the photo and slide it through the mail slot with our phone number and hope she calls if she recognizes him.

Kaleb and Porter both seem fairly enthusiastic about the idea, so it doesn't take long before we're back in front of her house. I run my fingers over the paper copy of the picture of our family before I open the mail slot and slide it through. My heart is racing, hoping beyond hope that she sees it and calls us.

"Stel, why don't we go get a hotel room? We can stick around for a few days and wait for her call; what do you think?" I nod and follow him back to the truck. I can't help but feel disappointed.

Kaleb gets us checked into a hotel about a mile from the house. We decide that for now we can bring our stuff up to the room and then get some dinner. When we get back to the main floor of the hotel something catches Porter's eye, he gasps and then runs in the opposite direction of the hotel exit.

"Porter, what?" I say frantically running after him. He looks back to me giddy and full of excitement pointing toward a glass door at the end of the hallway.

"They have a pool! Can we go? Please?" He folds his hands in front of him as he begs. Kaleb jumps in before I can respond.

"Well, I don't know. Do either of you have swimsuits?" He crosses his arms in front of him.

"No." Porter and I both say in unison.

"Well, unfortunately, bud, we can't go swimming without swimsuits." Porter sighs and looks at the floor, very obviously disappointed and begins to mumble under his breath. "I guess that's just a problem we're going to have to solve!" Kaleb chuckles when Porter's face instantly lights up at the idea.

"You mean it?" He's giving Kaleb his irresistible puppy dog eyes, and Kaleb chuckles and nods.

"I sure do, let's go get those swimsuits!" Kaleb and Porter excitedly lead the way. Quickly Kaleb turns back around toward me and winks, I smile back at him grateful.

* * *

I slip on my red swimsuit that Kaleb bought for me earlier and make my way into the pool room to join Kaleb and Porter who are already there. As much fun as it looks like they're having in the pool I make my way to the hot tub. Relaxing in the warm water sounds like a much better time to me at the moment.

I'm hoping that relaxing a little will help clear my mind of all the thoughts of today. It's hard not to wonder how this old woman connects to my dad, if she does at all. Maybe she's family?

I don't remember his parents at all or what they look like. So, she could maybe be my grandmother. I have no idea, what I do know however is that we've been hitting dead end after dead end. The phone number I have for him goes to voicemail every time, nobody seems to know where he went when he left and we're still working on charging the old phone we found in Judith's box.

I lean back in the hot tub and allow the water to engulf me. For once, I allow myself to dream of this happiness to continue. I don't need a whole lot of money or an expensive house or car. All I could ever want is here with me in this room.

I look up at them at the thought and watch as they splash water back and forth at each other. I love watching Porter play and be a kid for once. I slowly make my way out of the hot tub to join them in the pool and realize I need to use the restroom. I motion to the boys and let them know where I'm going.

I make my way down the little hallway and through the locker room. The bathroom is quite clean. It seems like Kaleb picked a pretty nice hotel for us. There's just certain things in here like the soap brand and the paper towels that lead me to believe that the hotel is a little nicer than some.

"Girl, I love your swimsuit!" I hear a voice echo from behind me. I turn around and there's another girl standing behind me in workout clothes. I look down at my wet body and red swimsuit. "That color looks great on you!" I blush and smile at her.

"Thank you." I stumble out before I quickly make my way back to the pool. Right before I round the last corner, I hear Porter's voice. It seems like he's trying to talk quietly, but his voice echoes across the water filling the room.

"Kaleb? Can I tell you a secret?" His voice sounds unsure and almost guilty. I feel like I should either go back into the bathroom for a few minutes or make myself known; I just can't seem to get my feet to move.

"Sure bud, what's going on?" Kaleb sounds concerned of course.

"You promise not to tell Stelly?" I can hear Kaleb thinking from here.

"Well, here's the thing bud, I'm always going to be honest with you. So, I need you to know that yes, I can keep a conversation between us private, as long as what you tell me does not interfere in any way with Stella's ability to keep you safe and to take care of you. Does that make sense?" There seems to be an awkward silence for a moment and then Kaleb adds "Because just the same way that I will be honest with you, I owe the same respect to your sister." Porter seems to understand because he begins talking.

"Well, you know how much I love Stelly and I know that she has done more for me than anyone else. I just, I can't help but wish that Judith were not so mean, you know? I just wish that she could be a mom to us sometimes. I want her to love me. I'm so stupid." It sounds like Porter is crying, I can't tell from here. However, his words are like a punch to the gut. How could he feel anything other than hate or anger for that monster? I'm not enough for him? He doesn't deserve to not be loved by his own mother, yet his words still hurt.

"Buddy, you are *not* stupid for feeling that way, no matter how it is. I want you to remember that feelings are not wrong, they're just feelings. It's about how you do or don't act on them. Do you understand?" Silence. I'm guessing Porter nodded. "Good, because you are a good kid Porter, full of love and light. Remind me later, I have something I want to give to you." There's silence again. I wait about another minute and then walk out from behind the wall.

"You guys have to check out those bathrooms! They're pretty nice! You picked a pretty great hotel, Kaleb, thank you." I smile and wink at him, he nods and smiles back.

* * *

Later that night Kaleb took Porter aside and pulled an old battered pocketknife from his pocket and gently placed it into Porter's small hand. He explained to him that he'd had it since he was young, that he got it right after his mom passed away. He told him that it was something physical that he was able to hold when he was missing her.

Kaleb told Porter that it was now his and to carry it with him everywhere, that it was an emotional symbol for him but that it was also a handy and useful tool to keep with him. Kaleb then laughed and told him that they'll probably need to get it sharpened though.

We spend the next few days exploring Seattle, enjoying ourselves and our time together. Every day I call the phone number in the morning and in the evening. Every time it goes straight to voicemail. I'm starting to think the phone number is a dead end too. Every day I also double, triple check that the sound is on, on my phone in case that lady calls, however I've yet to get any calls.

I pull out my phone to make the first call of this morning to the phone number and it rings before I have the chance to dial the number again. I answer the call right away and put it on speaker.

"Hello? This is Stella."

"Girl, you need to learn to speak slower. Are you the one that left this picture here with me?" I ignore her first comment.

"Yes, that was me!"

"Why are you putting a picture of Judtih through my mail slot?"

I'm confused, Judith?

"What? What do you mean? I was hoping you might know something about the man next to her, the one that I circled." She scoffs sounding annoyed.

"No. I don't know that man. Why were you here? What do you want?"

"Well I've been searching for him and in my searching, your address came up as one of his." She grumbles under her breath in obvious irritation.

"Child, does this have something to do with Judith showing up here years back asking to use my address as a mailing address?"

199

Now, I'm so confused. I look to Kaleb and Porter. They both look just as confused as I am.

"I honestly don't know. How do you know Judith again?"

"I don't really, she used to live next door twenty years ago. The last time I saw her was maybe ten years ago, she came by and asked if she could use my address as a mailing address. I asked her why and she told me she couldn't tell me just that it was important. I trusted her, so I told her it was okay."

None of this makes sense.

"So you don't recognize the man next to her at all?"

"No. I already told you that. Are we done?" I stutter for the moment, and I can't think of anything else to ask her.

"Yes ma'am, thank yo–" The phone clicks and the dial tone sounds through the truck. "Well, what do we do with that?" I look at Kaleb and he looks just as confused as me. Our only clue that brought us to Seattle is another dead end. Slowly we pack up the hotel and make our way to the truck.

I open the glove box and see Judith's extra phone in there. I pull it out and plug it in hoping it turns on this time. We tried charging it as soon as we got it, and it didn't work. We tried a few times until we just took it to a phone store, and they told us the charger was busted.

We just got this new charger yesterday, it was the only one he had and it was a car charger. I wait to see if there's any sign of life. Maybe we'll get some kind of a clue from it on our drive back.

Kaleb finishes putting our things into the back of the truck and then helps Porter into the cab. He looks at me almost as if he's reluctant to put the car into drive. I instantly understand how he feels.

Kaleb does put the truck into drive however, and when he does I realize that I never called the number we got for John this morning because the lady called before I could. I pull out my phone and hit redial on the number I had called many times in the last couple days.

Bzzzz bzzzz bzzzz...

I look up at Kaleb confused.

"Do you hear that?" Kaleb just looks at me with wide eyes as I reach down and pick up Judith's phone that was finally charged.

The screen was lighting up and the phone number displayed on the screen was mine.

Chapter Sixteen

We only have a few days left until Judith comes back, I can feel the disappointment devouring the space around the three of us as Kaleb continues to drive the truck toward home.

Judith's phone was completely blank aside from my most recent call to it. All we learned was that we now definitely don't have a way to contact him. About thirty minutes ago we were driving out of the hotel parking lot in Seattle and starting our four- and half-hour drive back.

We really found nothing. The only thing I know for sure now is that Judith knows more than she's said and that she had something to do with him leaving. I look at Porter who only a few days ago was smiling and laughing with Kaleb and me, is now sitting between us with his head hanging toward his lap.

Next to Porter, Kaleb is staring straight ahead eyes wide and keeping a death grip on the wheel, as if he's terrified of the road in front of him. To think that this is how we're ending what was probably the best summer for both Porter and me, makes me sick.

I move my elbow up to the bottom of the window so I can lean my head against my hand while I stare out the window. As the car speeds down the road, the trees become a green blur, my eyes begin to lose focus. A yellow sign with blue writing sticks out and catches my eye.

WILD WAVES theme park
IN 1 MILE!

The sign sparks an idea, if we can't go back with our goal finished, then we can at least head back having had a good day. One last good day of the summer.

"Kaleb! Take this exit!" Kaleb jerks the wheel a little, obviously startled by my yelling, blinks a lot and looks around confused for a moment with the exit now coming up right at that moment.

He realizes this last minute and jerks the wheel of the truck again just barely making the exit. I can see his heart racing as he pulls over, puts the truck in park and both Porter and Kaleb look wide eyed, filled with worry.

"Stel, what's wrong?" Kaleb is the first to speak, his hands shaking, barely noticeable to an unfamiliar eye, however incredibly obvious to me.

I scrunch my nose up in a sorry smile trying to say to them that there was no danger or anything and that I was sorry for scaring them. I start to laugh a little and then smile for real.

"Stel, what the hell?" I lift my arm and point to the bright yellow sign staring at us from across the intersection.

"Let's have fun today." I continue to smile at them when Kaleb's shoulders finally drop their tension and he is now smiling big at me.

"That's a great idea." He puts the car in drive and then tussles Porter's hair next to him who is still very obviously confused by what is going on.

I can feel myself getting a little nervous as he pulls into the water park, I've never been to one, I have no idea what to expect. I look over to Porter who is now realizing where we are, his face instantly lights up. He then looks up at me in surprise and excitement.

"No way! For real Stelly?" I nod and he throws his hands in the air in excitement jumping up and down in his seat.

Kaleb parks the truck and we make our way to the entrance. I look down at the swimsuit in my hands and then up at Kaleb, grateful to him for buying both Porter and me a swimsuit for the hotel pool. I lean into Kaleb's side so he can wrap his arm around me and then I squeeze Porter's hand that's enclosed in mine.

It takes us no time to change and for Porter to run into the first pool he sees, which just so happens to be a wave pool. I grab Kaleb's hand and run in after Porter.

The water is cold at first, washing goosebumps up my legs. I ignore the mild discomfort and plunge into the water with Porter, focused more on the joy in his eyes than the chill in my legs.

I splash him and then he splashes me back and soon enough we're mid water fight when Kaleb comes from behind me picks me up and tells Porter not to worry and that he's got his back. I start squirming in his arms laughing and laughing as he walks us deeper into the pool and then throws me into the water.

My body sinks into the depths of the pool. I almost start to panic, knowing I can't swim when I feel Kaleb's hand still holding tight to mine. I relax and as if it were nothing, he pulls me up out of the water and into his chest. My heart starts beating quickly once again at how close we are, his left arm wrapped tightly around my waist holding me tight against him. Our eyes were locked, both smiling ridiculously, faces only inches apart. Reaching up with his right hand he brushes my hair out of my face. It feels like we're the only two people in this pool right now.

"I could get used to this." We're still close enough that I can feel Kaleb's breath against my lips when he says this. My heart is beating so quickly, I'm sure he can feel it in his chest. He smiles gently down at me and I allow his bright green eyes to draw me in once again.

"Kaleb! Do me next! Throw me in next!" Porter's voice seems to bring both of us back to the busy pool filled with other people. Kaleb shakes his wet hair sprinkling me with water droplets and we both laugh as he walks us back to a depth where I can touch and sets me down.

Butterflies still fluttering around in my chest, I walk back until the water is shallow enough that I can sit down. Kaleb runs up to Porter and picks him up, like it's nothing and spins him around and then starts running him deeper into the pool like he did with me. He then throws him in and pulls him up and out of the water again the same way he did with me, this time, however he puts Porter on his back and walks him back to the shallow end.

I giggle as Porter runs around in the water laughing and splashing water around. He then runs up to Kaleb and asks him if he'll take him into the deep end where all the waves are. He then says he wants to swim with them like the other people are doing.

Kaleb and I both giggle a little, and as a response to Porter he picks him up and throws him on his back again. Kaleb looks back once as if asking if I want to come, and I shake my head laughing at Porter's 'woohooing.' Kaleb nods, smiling, and takes them into the waves.

I'm committed to not ending this summer on a gloomy note, I want to end it the way that it started. With fun, laughter and joy, just like one of the first lunches we took with Joe. I pull up the picture of that day that I saved in my mind and hold it there briefly. Opening my eyes, I take a picture of Porter and Kaleb laughing and smiling in between waves and save it in the archive of photo memories.

The two of them finally make their way back to me, Porter smiling and waving.

"Stelly did you see that?!" He yells to me in excitement.

"I did! It looked like you were having a blast kid!" He starts nodding over and over.

"It was sooooo much fun!" He giggles and then tells me he's gonna go run through the water streams that are spraying up from the ground. I accept his joy, letting it transfer to me as I cover my mouth and giggle to myself.

As Kaleb sits down, water splashes my leg next to me in little waves. I lean into him again, and in return, he rests his head on top of mine. My heart warms. There's not much that could beat a day like this.

"Stel?" Kaleb says while slowly lifting himself off and away from me. I look at him with evident concern spreading on my face.

"What?" I start preparing myself for the worst. He smiles at my worry, cups my cheek with his hand for a moment, pulls it away, and looks at his hands.

"Please don't be mad at me, and just in case our plan of finding your dad didn't work out, I've been talking with a friend of my uncle who's an attorney."

"What? So, you broke your promise! You said you wouldn't."

"Stel, stop." He puts his hand on my shoulder to calm me. "I never told him any specifics about you or Porter, just very vague details around the situation." He cuts himself off.

"That's not what matters; based on what I felt comfortable telling him, it sounds like if I got a bigger apartment and you planned to move in with me and had a job lined up, we'd have a pretty good chance of getting custody of Porter because of my income and already established place to live." My mouth won't move; it feels like I'm frozen; I don't even know what to say. Kaleb continues. "We would just have to prove Judith has said before that she doesn't want him and obviously the physical and mental abuse. As long as we do that, our chances are very good. The court usually tries to put a kid with family, and since you're his only family left aside from Judith, well–" I jump to him, wrapping my arms around his neck tightly.

"Thank you." Grateful tears begin to fall from my eyes and onto his shoulder. Kaleb pulls me back so that he can look at me. He wipes a single tear falling from my eye.

"Of course, Stel. I love you both. I would do anything for the two of you." Air sticks in my throat as I sit there breathless. Does he love us?

"You do?" The words come out a whisper from the lack of air in me. I grant myself a breath again until it's free flowing in my lungs and oxygen is flowing through me normally.

"Yes Stella. I really do." He rubs his hand on my cheek and I lean into it, closing my eyes.

"I love you too, Kaleb." *I always have.*

We spend a few more hours here, going down every water slide and into every pool. I make sure we experience every part of the park, because I'm not sure how soon we'll be able to come back.

The sun begins to set as we all climb back into the truck and Kaleb drives off. For a brief moment, I feel almost melancholy at the thought of today; it went by much too quickly.

I push the thought away and let in my gratitude for today that it was even possible. Shifting my gaze to Kaleb, I reach my arm over Porter and gently rub his shoulder.

"Thank you for making today possible, Kaleb." My hand falls down and around Porter's shoulder, pulling his little body into my side.

"Thank you for thinking of it." He winks at me and runs his hand through Porter's hair.

At this point, it was his signature move of affection with Porter, and the kid seemed to love it. He nestles his small body into my side and wraps his arm around my waist.

"Today was one of my favorite days ever Stelly. Thank you." Porter's voice begins to drop as his body slowly falls heavier into my side. I gently brush his hair from his face and bend down to kiss his forehead. *It was my pleasure kid.*

"You ready?" Kaleb asks this once it's obvious that Porter is deep in sleep.

"I have to be, don't I?" I take a deep breath when I say this. Kaleb gulps and then nods once.

"Remind me why we can't just pack up your things and bring them to my place tonight and have you both stay there with me until your birthday?" He sighs almost at the same time as I do.

We both notice this and each let out our own stifled laughs as not to wake Porter. I wish it were that easy.

"Because she's not just a drunk, she takes joy in our pain. If she came home and we weren't there, she would make sure to find us and getting custody of Porter would be that much harder because she would fight for him harder than she might if she didn't have time to think about it. If she has time to decide to be vengeful or time to purposely hurt us, Porter

211

might not live long enough for us to fight for him." All I know for sure is that nothing about this is going to be easy.

"I know Stel, I do wish it could be that easy." His body slouches slightly and he leans against the window with his right hand on the steering wheel.

"Me too." We spend the rest of the drive mostly in silence and I find myself drifting in and out of sleep a few times until I begin to recognize where we are.

I roll my window down and let the cold breeze hit my cheeks. I feel chills run through my body, and my stomach gets nauseous; something in the air tonight just doesn't feel right.

We turn the last corner off the main road and make our way into the trailer park. As soon as the tires hit the familiar gravel, my gut sinks again. My chest is pounding and as soon as Kaleb turns the last corner to where I can fully see our shitty little trailer, I know why.

Gerry's car is slowly backing out of the one parking spot in front of the shit box, and the kitchen light is on. She's home.

"Stel, what do you want me to do?" Kaleb is breathing quickly now, and I can tell that he's nervous. Porter slowly pulls himself off of me and sits up looking at me confused. At that moment I know that I have to handle this. We're about sixty feet from the trailer now.

"Park here." I unbuckle my seatbelt, pick Porter up, and plant him right next to Kaleb.

"I love you kid; I'll be right back." Porter looks more confused and starts to say something. I don't allow it. I'm now looking directly at Kaleb.

"Do not let him leave this truck until I tell you it's okay. Do you understand?" Kaleb nods and begins to say something, and once again, I don't allow it; before I know it, I'm outside the truck, jogging toward the trailer.

I don't know what's come over me, yet for some reason, I'm filled with determination.

Porter is safe with Kaleb. I can confront her without having to protect him. Now is possibly my one chance to find out what happened to my father and *maybe* what happened to my mother, too.

I swing the front door open, ready for anything, and step into the house.

She's standing in the kitchen, drink in hand, swaying back and forth, holding herself up against the counter. The smell of alcohol is stronger in here than it was two weeks ago.

"Well, well, look who it is." She waves her hands back and forth. "And where do you think you were? Do you know what time it is?" I ignore her satisfied anger and stand up straight, preparing myself to fight back.

"Hello, Judith."

Chapter Seventeen

Her clothes are disheveled and ripped in a few places. The ends of her hair is singed in a few places, probably from accidentally lighting it on fire, she probably shouldn't have tried a blowout.

Aside from her hair basically being too ruined for it to look good, it made it too voluminous, if you could call it that, for it not to be dangerous for her with her habits.

"Well, aren't you the brave one today? Don't have the little runt clutching to your hip, so you think you're invincible now? Don't worry, you'll get your ass beat with or without him, so why don't you just sit down and let it happen like the pathetic little bitch you usually are." She begins taking small slow steps toward me.

"No Judith, not today." Her face widens in shock, only for a moment, then it scrunches back into anger and then what looks like amusement.

Maybe if I can actually show her that I'm stronger than her here and now I could get her to leave us alone for the last few months we have to be here. If I no longer show fear of her, then maybe she won't try anything anymore. At least I know I can protect Porter the last few months.

"Excuse me?" Her mouth lays open for a moment still holding the look of angry amusement. She's no longer shocked at my resistance, in fact she's enjoying this, like it's a new little game for her.

"I'm not scared of you anymore!" I yell at her hoping it surprises her again. It does not. In fact, it seems to egg her on, she lifts the bottle in her hand as if to throw it and I flinch. Instantly, I know I fucked up when she starts laughing uncontrollably.

"You're not scared?! Then why did you flinch?" She says this smiling and moving her head back and forth mocking me.

Psychotic laughter spills from her mouth again. "You're fucking pathetic! Of course you're still scared of me." Mockery filling the air again. Her body slowly slinks over to me and she wraps her arm around me looking down, pinching my cheek.

"Don't you worry, mommy's only gonna hurt you a little." Her hand smacks against my cheek as she begins laughing again. Anger fills my chest this time and I push her off of me.

"No. No more!" My voice, louder now than before. She's still stumbling backward from my push against her. Her hand lands on the kitchen counter and she balances herself.

"You little cunt." She has daggers directed at me now and it looks like she's about to charge.

"No Judith, I have a few questions for you." My words fall on deaf ears, and she lunges at me and for the first time when her body reaches mine, she almost feels weak against me.

We struggle for a moment each gripping the other tightly pushing back and forth until I plant my foot behind me and swing her body toward the couch, shoving her down onto it. Shock once again fills her face, and just like before it stays around only briefly, she's angry again and tries to get up.

"What the fuck do you think…"

"Shut up." The words come out much more firmly than I thought they would and surprisingly enough this time Judith is now intrigued again. She sits back against the couch and crosses her arms as if to say she was listening.

I ignore her expression and move on, I still need answers.

"Judith, I know that you've been lying about something, probably everything but specifically about my dad, things just aren't adding up and none of it makes sense!" Instantly her face changes, and now she's very obviously pissed again. She's now sitting up straight like she's about to get up off the couch. Her eyes narrow toward me.

"How *dare* you bring him up to me! You are–"

"Just stop *LYING!* Where is he, Judith? What do you know? Did you do something? Is that why you lie about him? Are you the reason he's gone?" My voice is loud once again. I brace myself expecting her to come at me, and when I look at her, I almost don't recognize her. For the first time in a long time, I see fear on her face.

"How did you– no, NO, you know nothing! How could you?" Her voice raising and lowering all in the same sentence. A sentence that makes no sense, she continues. "But if you do know something." She snaps her head toward me, her eyes narrow and she stands up with certainty. "Well, we just can't have that. If I go down, well you'll just have to go down with me." She starts laughing again and instead of walking to me she walks right past.

"Wha-What are you talking about?" I say and watch her intently, trying to figure out what she's doing. She then picks up the full bottle of her 126 proof rum on the counter, takes a big swig and then walks to the back of the trailer.

I hear her mumbling and what sounds like liquid hitting the floor. She walks back into the kitchen from the bedroom except with the bottle upside down now facing the floor. She tips it up, takes a swig again and then turns it upside down and starts pouring it on the floor walking toward me, trailing it behind her as she twirls around in the living room. She splashes just about the last of it onto the couch and then mumbles something along the lines of not wanting to waste all of it. She then looks toward me again and starts shaking her finger in my face backing me up into the kitchen.

"You stupid, stupid girl, you thought you could win? You thought you could get one over on me, huh?"

I tried to understand what she was saying.

"You look confused, Stella, don't worry. You will understand soon enough." She pulls out the pack of cigarettes that were poking out of her pocket. She lights her cigarette and almost like it was in slow motion, she takes her first drag, and as the cherry brightens with her breath it all makes sense.

In the same motion, I lunge toward her to grab the lighter and cigarette, she takes what almost looks like a graceful step back when the door flies open and a panicked Porter is jumping into the trailer.

"Porter NO! GET OUT OF HERE!" I yell at him, still it's no use, Judith already has her arms wrapped around him and is throwing him toward me. She quickly steps to the front door to lock it and then faces toward the two of us.

I start thinking of a way to get Porter out of here and I remember the broken window in the back that would be big enough for both of us to fit through if I can knock out the metal frame. I start for the bedroom pulling Porter along with me.

"Look at that! Now we all get to go together. Oh don't run! Won't you watch with me?" She yells to us and I hear the familiar sound of her pulling the cigarette smoke into her lungs.

I look back once just in time to see her wicked smile directed right at me while she flicks her cigarette out of her hands landing right behind her. The floor is instantly consumed with fire in a loud whoosh. Judith barely escapes its grasp as she runs toward us. I slam the flimsy bedroom door behind us and lock it hoping it will keep her out long enough to knock out this window frame. Porter is standing in the corner of the bedroom terrified. I lean against the bed and balance myself so I can start kicking the window frame. I keep kicking and tell Porter that it's gonna be okay and that I'm gonna get us out of here. The window loosens a little more under my feet, I can feel that I've almost got it because I can hear the fire spreading deeper into the trailer.

"It's gonna be okay Porter, we're gonna be okay, I'm gonna get us out of–"

BOOM. The whole trailer falls to the left and I fall into Porter, both of us now leaning into the hot wall. I quickly get up and stumble back over to the window and start kicking again knowing that that was the first propane tank on the other side of the trailer and that we don't have much more time before the one on this side goes. I finally get the frame knocked out and see Kaleb running to the window yelling for both of us. I quickly spin around to grab Porter to hand him to Kaleb.

"Stelly!" Porter yells to me as Judith is now yanking him backward toward the door as fire starts filling this room now.

"Porter!" I reach toward him and try to pull him away from her, except she reaches around me and grabs my hair trying to pull me toward her as well. As I'm fighting to get myself and Porter free, I notice something shiny from the corner of my eye. The pocketknife Kaleb gave to Porter this summer.

Porter reaches up and cuts my hair free from her grasp and I fall backward and then before I can do anything Porter kicks me in the chest and I'm now falling out of the window that I just kicked out for *him*.

"NO!" I yell to him and as if every motion is moving one clip at a time, I see my arms and legs flailing in front of me and behind them I see the windowsill and my baby brother still inside wrapped in Judith's arms. They're both completely engulfed in flames, tears already burning their way down my cheeks. I see Porter one last time, and he's smiling at me, his mouth moving in a very familiar motion. 'I love you Stelly.'

My back hits the ground, blurry eyes, no breath coming I stand up to run toward the trailer.

I'm too late.

This side of the trailer is now engulfed and then.

BOOM!

My body is thrown backward and I land on my back again. I can't breathe, I can't get air in.

My head is pounding, my vision is coming and going, orange and then black over and over. I can't get air in. My ears are ringing, and pain is spreading all throughout my body.

It looks like a face is now in front of mine. I recognize it. He's yelling at me, and I can feel cold droplets hitting my cheek as he leans over me. I try to tell him that I can't breathe. Nothing comes out, just gasps of nothingness. I feel him shaking me, and with all my strength, I lift my head up and look toward the flames. I manage a "P—" before I lose my strength and fall back down.

"Oh my god! NO!" He jumps up and runs toward the orange screaming a name I know very well. What was it again? I can feel myself losing consciousness as I watch the boy pulling on the flaming metal and then I hear him screaming again as the darkness takes over again. The orange comes back and I can see another figure pulling on him and then the ringing comes back again.

Where am I?

Why is everything disappearing? My head slumps to the side as I let myself fade into the darkness.

Chapter Eighteen

There's red. Red, orange, white and it's hot, so, very hot. I feel a bead of sweat roll down my face and over my scar as I cough from the smoke. I can't move from where I sit, my body won't budge.

I'm stuck.

Sitting in the grass, pain flooding my body, barely conscious. The sweat drips onto my hand again, I look at it. A pool of dark red liquid lay across my knuckles. I look up unfazed, I'm all alone in a swarm of people, chaos all around me. The fire is blazing in front of me, uncontrollable. I can see what looks like people running around in front of me in orange and yellow clothing. It all blurs together.

I sit there watching as someone walks out of a cloud of pitch black smoke with someone slouched in their arms. Someone starts screaming, it's a dull scream to me. That's when I notice the ringing in my ears. For the longest time I can't pick out what she's saying, what anyone is saying, people are talking all around me, talking to me and it's all blurring together, I can't make out anything.

I'm sorry. Was that something someone was saying? Why? This was an *accident* right? What even happened? I shake my head confused. I look down at my hands and notice that they are shaking uncontrollably and someone else's hands are on top of them trying to calm them. It's not working. I followed these hands up to a face. Green eyes. His lips are moving, I can't make out what he's saying. I glance down slightly and the skin under his eyes look wet. I look down at his hands again and I notice this time that they are a dark red and covered in what looked like blood? Everything is still blurred. I'm so confused, why am I in pain, why am I sitting here in the grass? Why is my head pounding and why are my ears ringing?

Why?

I look up and I see him smiling at me.

It hits me.

Porter.

Everything comes rushing at me all at once and there's no stopping it. The first thing I hear is the unmistakable sound of sirens. Then people's voices start clearing in my head, asking me if I'm okay. They were asking what had happened and why?

The voices around kept telling me everything was going to be okay and that they were very sorry. As my mind tries to separate the voices around me, there's one voice missing and only one voice that I can very clearly focus on.

"I'm sorry! I didn't mean it! What are you doing? Why are you taking me away? Get off me, you piece of shit!" It's her. She's struggling against the medics trying to get her into the ambulance to take care of the large deep, dark red burn on the left side of her face and body. She won't let them. She continues to struggle like the crazy numb bitch she is.

This is when I finally remember exactly why I'm here and what's happening. I get up from the pavement and take a step and then another and soon I'm running. Then I stop, I stop right in front of her and her screaming halts.

"I'm sorry." She barely whispers almost as if it was a question. This is only the second time I have ever recognized the look of fear in her eyes. Every part of me wants to reach up and strangle her like the many times she's strangled me. I want to grab her by the hair and throw her head to the ground. I want to rip her heart out. I want to *kill* her. Murder this worthless piece of garbage. I don't do anything. I can't. I step back and turn toward the fire.

I hear a laugh from behind me as I watch the paramedics carry a black body bag past us and into a different ambulance. Pain floods my body.

"You've always been weak *Stella*."

I push all my emotions other than anger down and whip around and with all the force in my body, punch her as hard as I can. She looks shocked for a second and then begins laughing again as blood streams down her face out of her nose. Her head rolls back and then the rest of her body goes limp as she passes out.

The medics carry her into the ambulance and drive off. I turn around and start running for the fire. Hands immediately wrap around me and pull me into a pair of gentle, steady arms I can't break out of. I can't do anything.

Nothing. Not this time. All I can do is fall in his arms and scream, I cry too but mostly I scream, tasting the salty flavor of tears as they stream into my mouth.

I keep screaming the most blood curdling scream I can get out. My throat is raw, and I still don't stop, because it's the only thing I can do.

* * *

The first thing I notice is bed sheets underneath me, cold and crisp against my body. The next is the bright white light around me that's painful to look at. I squint my eyes for a while until I feel like they finally adjust.

My left hand begins to warm, looking down at it I notice a thickly bandaged hand on top of it. I look up to green eyes and my heart warms for a moment until I remember why I'm here.

I snatch my hand away and I can't help, but recoil at the sight of him now. I feel sick, nauseous at the thought. I can barely even think of the words without wanting to vomit. My mind goes there anyway, and I can't hold it back, I'm now leaning over the side of the bed spilling mostly bile all over the floor.

Images of this summer continue flashing in my mind, his smile and joy beginning to mix with the fiery image of the last smile I'll ever see of his. I can't seem to separate the images inside my head. It's all just spinning around in my head, making me dizzy, and it won't stop.

His bandaged hand reaches for me and I recoil again. This stops the spinning, my mind is now filled with red. My chest fills with hot anger. I look at him with hatred. How dare he show up here.

"How can you sit there trying to comfort me??" I spit my venom toward him. "This is *your* fault!"

"What? Stel, what are you saying?" I can see the pain spreading even more deeply than it was across his face.

"All you had to do was keep him in the fucking truck Kaleb, all you had to do was fucking listen, you couldn't even do that and now he's DEAD! DEAD, KALEB! You can't fix that! *Get out!*"

I feel tears running down my hot cheeks as my voice begins to break. His face is pulled together in all kinds of emotions, full of anguish. There's a part of me that wants to care. I'm just too full of rage right now, so I turn away.

"Stella, please, it wasn't that simple. Can we please talk?"

"Get. Out." That is the only thing I say. I can feel the slump of his shoulders. I still don't look at him, but I hear the swoosh of the curtain keeping the beds separate. I look back at the seat where he was just sitting, empty and still containing the imprints of him, having been sitting there for a while.

I allow myself to stay full of rage for hours because it's much easier than anything else. And, now that they are letting me out of here I'm not really sure what to feel. I walk out of the hospital and try to force myself to focus on the scenery around me instead of the feelings inside me. I focus on the sidewalk underneath my feet, then the trees that pass by me while I sit on the cold bus seat, and now the gravel underneath my feet and the line of ants trailing into the tree line.

My feet carry me forward out of memory until I'm standing in front of the burnt remnants of what was my home for so many years, yellow tape following the black burn lines on the ground.

I can no longer just focus on the things surrounding me because this time they were directly connected to my emotions.

Frozen in place something tickles the top of my shoulder, I reach my hand up and for the first time realize that my long dark hair is now gone and sitting at my shoulders. I remember why and feel the pain fill my chest and then take over my whole body as I slump to the ground, my knees slamming against the gravel. My eyes are now pouring with uncontrollable tears. I shiver as the breeze cools my wet cheeks. No sound comes out this time. I just stare at the wreckage, stuck in my silent pain.

My right cheek is all of a sudden filled with warmth, I reach my hand up and feel soft hair. I look over and it's Sadie, she gives me some more wet sloppy kisses. Behind Sadie is Joe with sadness spread all throughout his face.

Joe quickly walks to me as soon as my eyes reach his. He pulls me up off the ground and into his gentle arms. I cry in his embrace for a while before he leads me back to his trailer.

I sit down on his couch and I notice that I feel warm for the first time today.

Chapter Nineteen

Color is missing.

Where did it go?

Am I lost?

I can feel the empty space in my chest, the gaping hole screaming to the world that I am hollow. When the pain finally went away, it was never replaced with anything, creating a never-ending void that swallowed everything and absorbed nothing.

Logically I know that the seat beneath me is cold, my legs are covered in goosebumps and yet I feel nothing. My hand is resting against the windowsill in front of me gripping tight to the coffee cup that Joe brought me not too long ago.

Every few minutes my hand forgets that it's holding something, and the mug begins to slip until my brain reminds it of its job.

I hold the mug for a few minutes longer to please Joe and then I place the full cup on the table behind me. I never drink any of the tea he brings me anymore.

Every morning, I thank him, hold it for a while and then I set it down still full. I press my cheek to the cold glass and stare at the now empty dirt lot that used to be where I would hold him, protect him, love him.

I stare at the empty space and remember what used to fill the emptiness inside of me. He gave me everything and left me with nothing. He took everything with him when he left me alone.

The fire was on the news for a while, but it turned into just another tragic accident caused by addiction. People started using the story as a cause to fight addiction and I stopped listening because my story, really wasn't my story any longer.

My body as if on a timer turns toward the grassy area beneath the oak tree where we used to spend a lot of our time. For just a moment the sun catches my eye and it's as if I can see our ghosts sitting together under the oak tree again and then the sun is covered by a cloud and the ghosts are gone.

It's been about two months now since I've been staying with Joe. I didn't have anywhere else to go and he seemed happy to have me. Maybe not so much in the beginning, I'd wake up from the slightest sound out of habit and then everything would come flooding back. All the pain would overtake me, and I wouldn't be able to control it. Tears would escape me uncontrollably and it wasn't the silent sort of tears.

Within minutes Joe and Sadie would be next to me, Joe holding me in his arms and Sadie nudging my cheek and giving me the occasional kisses. This happened almost every night for about the first month. Then one night it was as if the tears just went away and so did everything else. The pain was replaced with a lack of feeling at all.

The world turned dull, nothing except grey.

The first month was intense, and Joe took a lot on when he took me in. However, I think Joe knew what it might be and chose to save me anyway. He was there when I found out Judith was going to prison, and he was there for all of the police interviews before and after that. And he was there for the funeral. In fact, if it weren't for Joe the funeral probably wouldn't have happened at all.

I didn't make it easy for Joe either, he wanted to do a celebration of life instead of a funeral and tried to explain to me that was what he did for his Laura, and I wouldn't have any of it.

Any time he mentioned it or tried to push for it saying that he thinks I'll be more appreciative of the celebration of life rather than the funeral later on. All I could respond to him was, *"What life?"* This always ended the conversation, eventually he gave in and planned a funeral instead.

I helped a little when he asked, it's just that I was so lost that I barely remembered to brush my teeth every day, let alone plan anything.

The funeral from what I heard and from the pictures that Joe so thoughtfully took for me knowing I wasn't all there, was very beautiful. That day went by for me as if it were in slow motion. Joe somehow managed to buy me a beautiful black dress that he said would still be just as beautiful with my black chucks.

At some point before the funeral, he also took me into a beauty shop for a proper trim. It was obvious to me at that point that he had daughters.

The morning of the funeral I was ready to leave without brushing my hair and apparently it had been all over the place because he sat me down, brushed it for me and gently pulled it back with a beautiful red ribbon telling me the color complemented my complexion and hair color.

There weren't very many people at the funeral that day, there were a few people who saw us passing from the trailer park, Sara was there and then Kaleb was there as well, however he wasn't there for very long.

I had noticed him briefly in the background leaning against a tree. He had his head down most of the time and when he looked up it was to wipe his eyes. I had then looked down at my hands for a moment and when I looked up again, he was gone.

Anyone who attempted to talk to me, I attempted to respond, but I remember just feeling so heavy, eventually I just sat down and stared out the window, ignoring the world around me the same way I'm doing right now. That was the first time I really noticed the hole in my chest. It only grew from there.

About two weeks ago I started getting calls from a random number, when I didn't answer eventually, he started leaving voicemails. It was my father's parents' attorney, every time he left a voicemail, he would just say that it was urgent and to please call him back at my earliest convenience, it had to do with my upcoming eighteenth birthday.

I'm not sure why my dead grandparents' attorney was calling me, I have had no interest in talking with him.

I'm not entirely sure that I have an interest in anything anymore.

It doesn't take long for me to come to the decision. I slowly lift my hand up to confirm my assumption and it was in fact correct. I don't see the color or beauty in much of anything nowadays and without that,

Without *Porter*?

What's the point?

Exactly.

There isn't one.

The void inside me is screaming louder than ever now and it's begging to join its family in nothingness.

Joe left not too long ago to do laundry so I know he'll be gone for a few hours. That gives me plenty of time.

Coming into full acceptance of my decision I begin to no longer feel any anger, in fact there's a calm that washes over me when I pull the bottle from Joe's medicine cabinet.

I take it with me into the living room along with a large glass of water. I lay down onto the couch so that I don't fall into an uncomfortable position for Joe to find me in. Gently I pull the red ribbon out of my hair and as I do this I notice in the shadows one last time the ghosts of Porter and me sitting under the oak tree.

The plastic bottle in my hand is cold and the prescription paper is peeling off slightly, almost like the bottle has been in the cupboard long enough for the condensation from the showers to ruin the paper. I pop the bottle open and pour its contents into the palm of my hand. I count out nine of the small white pills with the faint lettering on one side. **OC**.

I'm okay with this, there's nothing here for me anymore. I'd rather see what nothingness has to offer.

I pour the powdery little circles into my mouth, take a swig of the water and down they go. I lean deeper into the couch and make sure to tie the red ribbon around my eyes just in case my eyes don't stay shut, I don't want Joe to have to see the glossiness of the lack of life in my eyes.

It doesn't take long before I begin to feel sleepy. I can feel my heart rate begin to slow and right when I'm about to lose consciousness I hear the front door open.

Shit.

"Oh my god, oh no, baby girl."

I feel the gentle touch of his hand on my arm, and I smile my last smile at his warmth.

Pain.
Everything Hurts.
Again.

I thought I was leaving behind the pain. Light begins to flood through my eyelids, and I can feel them twitch at the brightness of it, not ready to open just yet.

"Stella girl?" His voice softens the pain slightly and I begin to fight to open my eyelids. It burns as soon as they do. I get dizzy at the brightness and have to blink quite a bit before I can see anything.

The first thing I see is a small body with blonde hair. I blink again and he's gone and in his place is Joe sitting in a chair next to me. His hand is squeezing mine.

"I'm so sorry honey, I never ever should have left you alone like that, especially this soon, I know better."

I quickly shake my head and squeeze his hand.

Relief.

It's a sudden feeling that washes over me with no warning. I can feel the gratitude that he found me in time growing inside of me.

I'm glad I'm still here to hold his hand again.

"I realize now, something I didn't before. I never wanted to die; I just wanted the pain to stop. I never wanted to have to live without Porter." I barely manage to squeeze this out before my body begins to shake and the sobbing takes control.

How am I supposed to live now? Porter... Tell me, how am I supposed to live now?

* * *

"Sweetheart?" A gentle tap on my shoulder. Joe. I reach up and run my hand across the red ribbon still holding my hair back when I turn to him. I kept the ribbon he had given me, and I wear it every day now.

I can tell how much it means to both of us. When we got back home from the hospital, he tied it in my hair again and told me that it can be a symbol for me moving forward, that pain can be beautiful too.

"I just wanted to let you know that Kaleb called again. Maybe you should go see him?" My initial reaction is to roll my eyes and I instantly want to take it back as soon as I do it.

I sigh.

"Maybe you're right." I shift uncomfortably in my seat at the thought of seeing him again. Joe and I have had some time to talk about what happened with Kaleb and I have some apologizing to do. I wasn't fair to him.

"Stella girl, you just need to be honest with him. He's not going to turn you away. That boy loves you very much." Joe winks at me and pats my hand as he says this. I let myself smile, even if it's just a little.

I can do this. Kaleb's is only about a twenty-five-minute bus ride from here. That gives me about twenty-five minutes to perfect what I'm going to say. I've gone over it many times. There are so many things I could say, I can never decide on one.

I stand up, nod to Joe nervously and head out the door.

The twenty-five minutes go by way too quickly, although I think I've figured out what to say. I'm just going to tell him that I shouldn't have treated him that way, there's no excuse and that I miss him and that I'm sorry. That's good, right?

UGHHH.

I knock.

The door opens.

"Hi." Is all I can get out before I forget all the things I thought of saying.

At first, he's shocked and that quickly changes to what seems like relief? I don't have any time to figure it out before he pulls me into his arms.

It seems I have the same reaction he had to seeing me at his door. I swing my arms up and around his neck pulling him closer to me. I pull him as close to me as I can, and it takes no time at all before I'm soaking his t-shirt with my salty tears.

I stand on my tiptoes, pulling him down to me *"I've missed you."* I say quietly into his ear that's, for the first time in months, so close to me again. He gently pulls away from me, but only just enough so that he can look at me.

"Stel–" He's gazing down at me tucking my now short hair behind my ear, still holding our bodies together. He leaves his hand resting on my cheek gently brushing the continuously falling tears out of my eyes with his thumb. His eyes are wet, and I can tell he has also been crying.

It's not hard to see the torment in his eyes, there's guilt there too. I'm so stupid and *selfish*.

Kaleb loved him too, and I've left him here all alone to grieve by himself. This time it's my turn to comfort him. I bring both my hands to his face the same way he had his hand on mine. I hold him like that for a moment staring up at him before I pull him down to me. I stand up on my tiptoes and pull him into my shoulder. I keep him pressed against me until I can feel his body start to shake as he begins to sob.

"I'm the guilty one, Kaleb, you didn't lose me, I *left* you." His sobbing gets louder, and I can feel him completely letting go.

We stand in his doorway for what seems like forever. Eventually we break apart and he welcomes me inside. His apartment feels different this time. Like it's missing something, or someone. I can tell he feels it too, I think about how he's probably felt it this whole time and I hate myself even more.

We both sit on his couch, neither of us saying anything. It feels almost like he also has a giant gaping hole in his chest and for some reason sitting in our emptiness together makes it feel like the void is, little by little, filling with something absorbent. I move closer to him and slide my hand into his. He squeezes my much smaller hand and we just sit like that, gradually filling each other's void.

After what feels like hours Kaleb looks at me and breaks the silence.

"So, your birthday is in a few weeks. I have something for you, and I'd love to come by to give it to you if that's okay?" I squeeze his hand one more time before I bring my hand back to my own lap and turn toward him.

"I–"

My phone rings. I want to ignore it and tell Kaleb that I would love that, but for some reason I have a feeling that I need to answer the call this time. I pull my phone out from my back pocket and as I guessed, it's the lawyer again. I tell Kaleb that I need to take it and flip the phone open.

"Hello?" The attorney clears his voice on the other end of the call.

"Hello, is this Stella Peterson?" He clears his voice again. I tell him yes. "Hi Stella, my name is Elijah Mintz." He then asks if my parents are John and Judith Peterson, again I say yes. As soon as I say yes again, he starts to sound very excited, saying he's so happy to finally get in touch with me and that he's been trying me for weeks, that he was worried he had the wrong number.

"I knew your grandparents for a very long time, I was their attorney for many years, they eventually became more friends than clients. I've been waiting a very long time to make this phone call and I am overjoyed to finally be hearing your voice." I'm amazed at how sincere he sounds in this conversation compared to his voicemails.

The tone of his voice however is only the beginning of my amazement during this conversation. He continues explaining to me that my grandparents loved me very much and almost every year before they passed, they would come in and add something more to their will for me if they passed before I turned eighteen. And every year they came in they would tell him how much they wished they could just see me in person but that for now, this will have to do.

He went on, that at least within a few days of my eighteenth birthday he would love to meet with me so we can go over the will together in person and we can get everything signed over to me.

The way he was talking was giving me anxiety because I didn't completely understand what he was saying. He kept mentioning that I would be getting something from their will, however he has yet to mention what. He keeps talking about these people loving me that I barely even knew.

"Wa–wait! I'm sorry, I guess I'm just having a hard time understanding, what exactly is happening?" I say cutting him off before I let myself become even more confused.

"Sweetheart, they left you everything. You're set for life."

Chapter Twenty

I'm officially eighteen today. I had waited for this day for so long, and now it almost feels worthless.

I left Kaleb's in a daze the other day and had to text him that night to tell him that I would love to see him today because I could barely walk straight after my phone call with Elijah.

I was swimming in mixed emotions. The one emotion I have not allowed myself to feel is excitement.

How *dare* I? I don't deserve any of it, if I had just been patient, if I had just waited. If I had told someone sooner! My grandparents might have taken us away from her so much earlier in his life. If only I hadn't been so selfish… *Porter would still be alive.*

It's my fault, Porter is gone because of me. I can't help feeling this way as I look at myself in the small bathroom mirror. I stare at my pale grey eyes, they stare back.

Stelly.

I whip my head around, I know that voice, yet I see no one. I open the bathroom door and look around the small trailer. Nothing. Thinking it must just be in my head, I go back to the bathroom and continue getting ready for the party that Joe insisted on throwing.

I look at myself in the mirror one more time, I kind of like the shorter hair on me. I allow a smile to grow on my face for the first time in a long time and instantly feel guilty letting the smile drop from my face.

Smile Stelly.

There it is again.

"Hello?" I swing the bathroom door open frantically. It's his voice. I know it. I look all around the trailer, and again, nothing, so I run outside and look all around the outside, and still nothing. I'm not sure what that was. I wouldn't mistake that voice for anything. Maybe I'm just finally losing my mind.

The party was really just Joe, Kaleb and me. They both did their best to make me feel special, and I did my best to pretend that I did. We played cards for a while, and Joe made us some burgers and tried his hand at some baking.

The cake he brought out was very obviously made by someone with zero experience in baking, and it was all the better for it. We eventually moved onto presents, which all of this was something I was very unfamiliar with.

Joe went first, passing me a gift wrapped by someone who also had very little experience in gift wrapping. I giggled a little and felt authentic doing it. I pulled back the last piece, exposing a beautiful handbound leather journal. It was much better quality than the one I had now and had much more blank space than mine. I made sure to hug Joe, thanking him for such a beautiful gift.

Next was Kaleb's. It was tall and thin like a picture frame, also covered in messy wrapping. I laughed this time, truly grateful to have these two men in my life. I gently pulled away the paper and underneath was not anything I ever could have expected. Tears instantly began running down my cheeks. Joe, sitting across from me, instantly became worried and jumped up to see what I was looking at. Almost instantly I could hear sniffles coming from behind me.

I looked back and forth between the beauty in front of me and Kaleb.

"How?" I barely choked out between tears.

He went on to explain that this was the night he actually found out we didn't live at the house he'd been dropping us off at, that he was going to approach me then, however when he saw us like this that night. He said he just couldn't interrupt us. He instantly fell in love with the image in front of him and went home that night and started the painting.

Before he can say anything else, I reach across the table and gently place my lips against his. I can taste the saltiness of my tears as they fall onto our lips. It's a bittersweet moment, I'm not entirely sure that this was the right time to kiss Kaleb for the first time, still my body became so overwhelmed with emotions that I wanted to feel something else. I lean back into my seat and look back at the painting.

The painting I was looking at was of Porter and me under the oak tree dimly lit by the streetlights. His small body was wrapped in mine as I read to him. I'm not sure what changed in that moment however I felt a sort of release. Porter and I did the best that we could.

"Kaleb, will you take me to see him?" I begin to feel almost comforted at the thought.

Kaleb helps me from his truck slowing the impact my feet make against the wet grass. I keep my hand in his as we walk along the path of the cemetery toward Porter. The air is cold and wet at the same time.

Light grey clouds filling the sky around us. Every surface around us was covered in light dew. I breathe in the smell of fresh cut grass and air that was recently greeted by rain. I squeeze Kaleb's hand in mine making sure he's still there.

Kaleb leads us off the path and before I know it, we're standing in front of a damp stone slab with my brother's name etched into it.

Porter J. Peterson
Beloved brother and friend
June 1993 - July 2003

It's surreal standing here in front of his grave this time. I wasn't really all there the last time I was here, and I'm not entirely sure what I'm even supposed to feel standing here. It's not Porter; it's just an empty coffin and a cold stone slab with his name on it.

I look up to Kaleb to see if he has any answers. He bends over and kisses my forehead and then hands me a bouquet of flowers that I didn't even notice he had. I squeeze his hand and lean into his chest before I take my hand back bending down, so I'm face to face with the gravestone.

I place the flowers on the ground in front of it and from the corner of my eye I notice something. On the bottom left corner of the gravestone is an oddly placed rock about the size of my flip phone. I reach down to toss it away from Porter's grave when I see some markings on it. I pick it up and sure enough someone has engraved J.P. into this rock.

I look up to Kaleb and he looks just as confused as I do. Curious, I place the rock back where I found it. Before I stand up again, I look back and forth a few times between the engraving on Porter's headstone and the engraving on the rock and that's when it clicks. I have no idea how it got here, but I know *she's* the one that had it put here. It all makes sense now. It was really the only explanation; I have no idea how I haven't thought of it before.

I quickly stand up. It's time I got some answers.

"Kaleb, I need to talk to Judith."

"What? Why??" Kaleb now looks even more confused than before.

"I have to ask her something." Not waiting for him I start to walk away when I feel a hand pull on mine.

It's not Kaleb's. It's a small hand. A hand I know very well. I squeeze down on the hand thinking that if I hold on tight enough it won't disappear, but as soon as I squeeze the feeling is gone. I flip around frantically searching for any sign of him, anything that says he was here just now. Seeing nothing I try to shake it off and start walking toward the truck again.

Be happy Stelly.

And at that, I understand. I know what he's saying. And *Porter* I promise, one day I will be, but I have to talk to Judith first.

Chapter Twenty-One

Judith
Ten years ago

I pace back and forth in the kitchen rocking Porter in my arms. I know he'll be home soon and based on his call earlier I can tell that he's upset.

I don't understand why he allows these thoughts to take him over like this. I feel like he knows deep down that I would never cheat on him, yet he allows all the anxiety to take over anyway.

I hate these arguments, but I *love* him, and I'll calm his anxieties every day if that's what he needs. Maybe one day he'll finally let it go and trust that I am and always will be faithful to him.

Porter finally drifts to sleep in my arms, so I gently place him in his crib. I feel a sort of relief that I won't be holding him when John gets home. I was focusing back on the dinner I had cooking in the kitchen when I hear the pitter patter of little feet running down the hall.

"Mommmmyyy!" Stella makes the corner into the kitchen almost too quickly, she slips a little, and then steadies herself. She thrusts her Polly pocket up toward me.

"Polly fell in half. You can fix her right?" I try my best to give her an encouraging smile when I check out the scene, she's right Polly is in half, however it looks like it will be a pretty easy fix.

I picked up Polly and her other half and pretend to struggle putting her back together when in reality I was able to pop her top half back into her bottom half almost instantly. I struggled for only a moment longer and then hand her back to Stella like it was magic.

Stella looks at me excited for a moment and then snatches her Polly back and disappears back into her room. I laugh to myself and head back into the kitchen.

The front door unlocks and then the door opens. I hear the pitter patter again of Stella's tiny feet.

"Daddy!" She screams in glee and I can hear the sound of her jumping into his arms.

"Hi baby," He kisses her forehead, and I can tell by the sound of his voice that he is definitely in one of his moods. I brace myself and do my best to just be kind to him.

He walks into the kitchen with Stella in tow. I can tell he's upset, but I can't quite tell yet which version I'm going to get.

Will it be the one who is ready to argue or the one that I have to pull answers out of just to get to the argument. I breathe in and then walk over to him like nothing's wrong and wrap my arms around his neck, holding him close. I kiss his cheek wishing that I could fix it for him with just a hug, that I could make it all go away just with a touch.

His touch always melted away any anger or frustration, all he ever had to do was hold me close and I'd melt in his arms. It wasn't the same way for him.

He needed to feel all his emotions, there was never any speeding it up with him. For some reason I would always try anyway. I know it's selfish, I just always want us to go back to us as fast as possible.

"Stella baby, could you go and tidy up your play room please?" I'm now bent down in front of her bright grey eyes that match her dad's and her dark brown almost black hair that matches mine. Her face is pouty but obedient, I brush my thumb across her soft cheek before she runs off down the hallway.

I stand back up and wait patiently to see where he takes this. I pick at my fingernails nervously hoping we can get through this argument quickly so that we can just have a nice night and a good dinner together.

257

"Judy, I don't know why I get like this, I just can't help but feel like you've been focusing your attention on someone else." My chest fills with pain, a fearful pain. Not fear *of* him, fear that he's going to *leave*, and that I won't be able to fix it.

"John I would *never*. I love you so much, and I love our family. I don't ever want to lose you and I would never do anything to risk that."

My words are not reaching him, he's already made his decision about this, he is so sure. I can feel doubt begin to fill me, not of my love for him, just that I can't fix it this time.

My chest is so hot, and I can tell that I'm also starting to get angry, mostly because he won't listen and I just want to be done so we can go back to the good part of us.

"I just don't believe you Judy, because you lie all the time." The sting of his words dug into my chest like I'd been stabbed.

I don't lie to him, not about stuff like this anyway. Any time I've ever lied it's been because I didn't want him to take an argument even farther or have even more weapons to throw at me than the ones he was already wielding.

I can feel the pain welling up inside of me, all the emotions trickling over. My nails are digging into my hands, and I want to scream because I feel like I'm not being heard and all my anger, frustration and hurt are pressing against my chest.

There's a hot burning sensation growing in my throat, it feels like there is a hot poker being shoved down my throat.

I need to let it out, I walk into the kitchen and look around and grab the first thing I can. A plate. I threw it on the ground. As soon as it shatters, tears begin rolling down my cheeks.

"I'm not lying to you! You know I would never do something like that! I could never hurt you like that." The tears just keep coming.

"Why do I not believe you?" I can now see that tears are also falling down his cheeks.

"I DON'T KNOW!" I feel so alone right now, he's not listening to me at all, and I get it he believes actions more than words, but I don't know what actions I did to create this doubt in him.

There's the burning sensation in my throat again so I pick up another plate and throw it, releasing more tears as it shatters. "I have given you no reason to not trust me."

"Oh really? And what about all those late nights you spent at the office with that guy at work, almost exactly twelve months ago?!"

I feel like I'm about to lose it on him because this is just getting ridiculous, I just want it to be over.

"Oh my god. Are you serious? You know that was work! And it's not like WE weren't trying!" The heat of the iron poker is back again, but I'm out of plates so I just let it burn.

"I just—" John starts to say something, and more tears fall down his cheek before he can finish. "I can't do this right now; I need to get out of here." He walks over to me and kisses me on the forehead and then turns away. No, no, no. Please don't leave. I'm about to run after him when I see Stella's tiny little body running after him instead and I freeze in place.

"Daddy no! Where are you going?" Stella is now yelling at him and crying with a death grip on his pant leg. He looks down at her with sad eyes and then bends down to meet her.

"Sweetheart, you know how much I love you right?" She's nodding tears off her face. "Well, baby, I have to go away for a little bit, but I will be back for you. I promise, I will come back for you." He strokes her cheek and gives her a sad smile, a tear falling over his lips. "I love you so much." He says this to her with more tears trickling down his face as he stands up and looks at me.

"Goodbye, Judith."

No.

No.

No.

No.

Please don't leave me.

I feel like I'm choking on my words. They burn in my throat leaving the taste of ash.

He turns away and walks out the door, car keys in hand. Stella looks to me for answers and I can't even keep myself standing anymore. I crumple on the floor.

"Mommy, what's going on?" Stella looks at me terrified, I still can't get words to come, so I just motion her toward me. She jumps into my arms, and I sit with her like this until she falls asleep and the pain in my throat finally cools and settles back into my stomach.

I put Stella in her bed and bring Porter's crib into her room and place him next to her.

The glass in the kitchen is everywhere so I start cleaning it up when I hear the lock on the door unlatch. Hope fills my chest. Maybe he's calmed down and everything can go back to being good again.

A pile of glass shards in front of me I wait impatiently to see what the energy will be. To my disappointment it seems like he is still upset.

I run over to him and wrap my arms around him anyway. I'm just glad that he's home so that we can get through this. He shrugs me off him and walks past me into the kitchen to grab some water.

"Please John, please don't leave me. Please can we just move past this argument?" Tears begin to fall again, and the burning of the heated iron poker has reared its ugly head again.

"Judy I'm done, I can't anymore. I just don't trust you."
It takes everything in me not to scream out in pain.

"No, please I can't lose you." I'm now gripping his jacket
trying to hold him here with me.

"Judy get off of me." He pushes me away from him. I feel
helpless against the rage that's boiling in me.

"No John! You can't leave me!" I smack his chest in anger.
How dare he?

My push barely moves him, yet it's enough for him to
take a step back and when he does he steps on the broken glass
on the floor and before I can do anything, he's lost his balance
and is falling backward. I reach out to grab him, to catch him,
but it's no use. His head smacks hard against the corner of the
kitchen table.

Silence.

He's unmoving on the floor in front of me.

Oh god no. I rush over to him.

"John, John." My hands are gripping his shirt and
shaking him. "No, no, no, no, no. John!"

Nothing.

His body lay there like a puppet whose strings were cut.
His eyes are wide open and no longer blinking and it's almost
like a glassy film has grown over them. I place my finger under
his nose and feel nothing so I place my fingers right under his
chin on his neck. There's still no movement. I quickly rack

my brain to remember how to do CPR. They had us do a class a few years ago at work.

I remember and immediately get up and lean over him and place one hand over the other. I press down on his chest counting to fifteen and then open his mouth and breathe in twice. I keep going like this for what feels like hours. Nothing is changing and he still has no pulse. A loud cracking noise booms through the house and it feels like my hands fall through his chest. I freeze unable to keep going after I just cracked his ribs.

I realize then that he's dead.

And it's *my* fault.

"Oh god... No John..." My head smacks the ground before I even realize that I'm falling.

I can't control any part of my body anymore and the sobs start coming in waves. I'm stuck on the floor like that for at least an hour until all of a sudden the smoldering in my throat burns so deep the pain turns dull and then I'm just stuck frozen in place.

It almost feels like my mind knew that I couldn't handle the pain and so it just turned everything off.

I can feel myself slowly desensitizing more and more until finally.

I'm numb.

One hour.

Two hours.

Three hours.

I blink and a stinging ache spreads through my eyes like they were completely dried out and my eyelids were scraping across them. I blink a few more times until my vision clears.

I need to call for help. I scramble to my feet to call 911 and then my hand stops, hovering over the phone when I remember.

There's no longer a reason to call for help.

I look around the dark room and realize that at this point I only have a few options here.

Option one I call the cops and tell them what happened. More than likely I will be arrested and knowing John's parents I will probably spend the rest of my life in prison and they will raise Porter and Stella.

I shake my head. No.

Option two… I call the cops and tell them I came home and he was like that. Nope that won't work. I will still get arrested, and John's parents will hire an outrageously expensive lawyer and once again. Prison. They raise the kids.

Option three… I call one of the attorneys at one of the offices we work closely with and hope that they help me and don't turn me in. That could work, but I have no money to pay them and I just started as a paralegal. Plus, I'd be asking them to what, help me get rid of a body? I doubt they would give me the time of the day without the money. Again. Prison.

Option four, I get rid of his body and clean up the mess. I'll use his phone and text his parents and Paul and tell them that things aren't working out with me and that he has to get away from here. That he needs to start a better life for himself somewhere else. I'll also tell them not to try and change his mind and that they probably won't hear from him for a while and that he's going to get a new phone and he'll reach out when he's ready. I think I can make this work.

Looks like it's option four.

I look up at the clock.

Twelve am.

Okay, sunrise is in about six and a half hours. That means anything that I need to do outside needs to happen immediately. I don't know much, I haven't been a paralegal for that long, but I just recently helped one of the attorneys with a murder case.

Thoughts are swimming around in my mind. *Stop!* I need to focus on one thing at a time. What were the main things the cops looked for when investigating? I look down at my hands, they are shaking uncontrollably.

First, I need to get him wrapped up so that I can drag him out of here.

The weirdest part about all of this is how calm I am while I roll my husband's lifeless body onto his tarp that he used for camping that he kept in the garage. Out of breath, I bend down for a moment and out of nowhere a memory of our wedding pops into my mind, when he's telling me that I will always be the only one for him. The way his lips tasted against mine when he kissed me in front of our friends and family. The saltiness of our happy tears spilling onto our mouths

I taste salt on my tongue and realize I've been stuck in a daydream, mouth gaping with tears falling down my face. I quickly wipe them away and focus back in on what I'm doing. I drag the tarp to the door.

I take a moment to breathe before I have to finish this and drag him out to the woods Stella plays in. I look at the tarp and my stomach churns. I can't stop it, before I know it I've thrown up all over myself and all over the floor.

I quickly begin to clean it up and then strip naked and put my clothes into a pile and throw out the paper towels.

The hot water on my body feels amazing at first until I look down at my feet and my vision gets spotty. My stomach churns and I lean against the shower wall, now light-headed. This turns into nausea and I can't hold back the vomit that spills out of me again and onto the floor and some of the wall of the shower.

I steady myself knowing that I still have a long way to go tonight. I wiggle my toes against the white shower floor beneath me in the warm water one last time before I get out and dry off.

I tie my hair up tight against my head and then wrap it in a t-shirt so as to not shed any excess hair or DNA and then throw on some jeans and a t-shirt I don't care about and then a pair of gloves.

As I make my way back into the living room, I start brainstorming how I'm going to drag him out into the woods when an image of Stella's red sled they use in the winters pops into my head. I scurry to the garage and grab the sled and John's climbing gear. I know he has some rope in there that I'll be able to use.

It takes me a while, but I finally manage to drag him out to the woods behind the house where Stella and Kaleb always play and where we buried our old dog Bruno. I stop using the sled right in front of Bruno's grave and decide that I'll have to carry John the rest of the way. It feels almost impossible, but I get John's body over my shoulder and I walk until I feel like I can't walk anymore and begin to search for a rotting tree with a hole big enough for John to fit into. I see one that will work about six feet ahead.

I stumble the last stretch completely out of breath. As best I can, I flop him into the hole and shove him back until I can no longer see him. Still wrapped in the tarp, I cover him in a thin layer of dirt.

I grab as many sticks and rocks as I can, things that are a little harder to dig through and I throw those on top of him as well. I'll drive down the road a little later and pick up some fresh roadkill to put in front of the stump as well. When I feel like he's covered as best as I can get him I walk back to Bruno's grave and realize that in all the chaos, Bruno's gravestone that Stella made him years ago was knocked down. I gently put it back into place.

Shit.

Stella, what am I going to tell her? There's no story in this situation in which it doesn't sound like he just got up and left her. I shake my head. I can't think about this right now.

When I finally make it back into the house I walk inside and check the clock.

Four thirty three.

That means I have two hours to finish up. That's doable. I can't get the thoughts out of my head that maybe John's parents were right. Maybe we never were good for each other. Maybe they had a good reason to hate me. Just not the reason they thought. I was never in it for the money. I just love John.

Loved.

Either way they never would have allowed me to be free if they found out about this. They would make sure I got blamed saying it was planned, so I could get ahold of his money. *Their* money. Well, jokes on them. I don't want it.

I wrap up cleaning in the living room, knowing that the hardwood will be slightly ruined after using bleach, I drop the bottle on the floor to create a story that I dropped it on my way to clean the bathroom one day.

`It's officially light outside and my body is exhausted. I grab my cigarette stash and slump down to the floor in the kitchen.

I light the cigarette and breathe it in, allowing it to fill my lungs and calm my anxiety.

I am a horrible human being.

I don't know how I'll ever be able to look at those kids the same. I'll never be able to look at them and not feel guilty. And worst of all, I'll never be able to look at them and not see John. The love of my life. Who's dead because of me.

Breathe in.

Breathe out.

The kitchen begins to fill with smoke and my body once again goes numb. I don't fight it; I just allow myself to slowly dull out until all I can see or focus on are the clouds of smoke filling the air in front of me.

Nothing matters anymore.

I smile to myself at the thought of nothingness as I breathe out another cloud of smoke.

Chapter Twenty-Two

"Well, Stella, now you know everything." I can't control the obvious shock on my face. Not just about what happened but that the woman that I grew up with, that I always thought was lazy and stupid, managed something so detailed, and *got away with it!*

It just proves to me that at the end of the day she's even worse than I thought she was, because the life we had was what she chose for us.

It was a selfish choice, one to protect herself and not her kids. I can't help but wonder if maybe I should have just stayed away. And every time I land on the answer that I never would have been able to let go of the curiosity.

She is and always will be the horrible monster I've never known. I stand up and push my chair in.

"Judith, thank you for being honest for once, however you are still a monster to me, and you always will be. You took two of the most important people from me and I will *never* forgive you. But I'm letting you go. I'm letting it all go. I no longer have room for you in my life or space for you in my mind. So, this is where we say goodbye, you will *never* see me again." I don't stick around for a response, because I don't need one.

For the first time, I feel like I'm finally free of her, finally free of the fear.

I'm finally free.

When I walk outside Kaleb is leaning against his truck tapping his leg nervously waiting for me. I smiled and run to him *finally* ready to enjoy every moment given to me. Ready to be *happy*. He's surprised but readies himself right away, opening his arms for me to jump into and I do. I lean back, grab his face in my hands and pull his lips to mine.

"Let's go home." He looks at me surprised.

"Home?"

"Yes," I giggle at the curious half-grin on his face. He squints at me for a moment, still smiling, and then seems to surrender to me.

"Alrighty then, lead the way." And I do.

* * *

I had Kaleb stop at Elijah's office on the way so that I could sign all the necessary paperwork and get all the information I needed from him.

Apparently, I was now the owner of a million-dollar house deep in the forest, a few different stocks, other assets, and a 1965 Porsche 911.

Elijah also helped me set up a bank account so that $15,000 would be deposited into it for me each month. He also promised that he would help me figure out all of the financial stuff so that I didn't have to worry about it.

When we finally reach the address Elijah gave us, it's almost hard to believe it's now my house. It is truly the most beautiful house I've ever seen. The inside did not disappoint either. There's a huge kitchen that opens to the living room and there's even a fire pit and a hot tub in back. The best part about the property though was the massive amount of land and the beautiful view in the back.

My body suddenly fills with the urge to do something. To just enjoy. I grab Kaleb's hand and drag him outside with me. I rip off the cover of the hot tub and not only is it full of clean water but it doesn't need to be warmed.

Thank you Elijah.

I undress to my underwear and get in as fast as I can. I let out a sigh as I feel my toes that were tingly only a moment ago begin to thaw and warm in the water. I run my hands over the top of the water doing my best not to break the surface.

I look up and Kaleb is just standing there staring at me in what looks like awe.

"Well? What are you waiting for? Get in!" I giggle as he instantly undresses and hops in with me. A few minutes go by before I realize Kaleb is staring at me. "What?" I laugh through the question.

"You found her again and brought her back to me." I look at him confused, and he just brings his hand to my cheek and holds me steady. "My best friend, my Stella, the one who took me on adventures and inspired me to be creative and got me excited about made-up games in the woods."

"Hey! They weren't made up if we played them." I giggled and then winked at him. He just kept looking at me with a longing to his expression.

Suddenly, he's bringing his other hand up to my face and pulling me toward him. His lips crash against mine and I can tell by the way he's kissing me that he's desperate for more. I go along with it, because so am I.

He moves his hands from my face down to my waist and pulls me into his lap. I wrap my legs around him and run my fingers through his hair. My heart is racing as he moves his lips from my lips to my neck. I pull his face back up to mine so that I can look into his eyes. I take control and gently touch my lips to his, enjoying every moment of their tenderness. I wrap my hands around his neck and pull him as close to me as I can.

Kaleb grabs my waist and pushes me back against the wall of the hot tub, and just as he's about to kiss me again, the doorbell rings. I sit up, shocked.

"Please, just ignore it for now." He pleads with me, but I smile at him as if to say, sorry, not this time. His head drops in disappointment as I climb out and wrap myself in a towel from the cupboard on the deck.

I open the front door and standing in front of me is an older lady holding a plate of cookies. She smiles brightly as soon as she sees me.

"Oh, you must be Stella, you look just like your father you know."

"Wha–"

"Excuse my manners, Stella, my name is Ingrid, Ingrid Picalo. I live only a few houses down, and when I saw a car that wasn't Mr. Mintz's pulling into this house, I figured it had to be you." She went on to explain that she's lived here a very long time and watched my dad grow up in this house and was very close with my grandparents. She also explained that she promised them she would look after me if they were no longer here when I turned eighteen.

There are so many people that loved either me or my dad or both of us, that I didn't even know existed. I tell Ingrid that I'm so grateful she stopped by and that we'll have to get together sometime soon.

Gratitude washes over me as I walk the plate of cookies from Ingrid over to the kitchen counter. It's not long before Kaleb is right behind me with his steady arms wrapped around my waist.

It's a weird thing to be free. I'm still not entirely sure what all the emotions are that I'm feeling. What I do know for sure is that I will keep my promise to Porter.

"Stel, you, okay?" Kaleb bends over to look at me and smiles, pulling my hands into his. "You look a little out of it." Kaleb is always so concerned when I space out, but honestly, it's nothing to be concerned about, in fact it's the opposite because I finally feel safe enough to do it.

I squeeze Kaleb's hands and then look into his green eyes that I helplessly fall into every time. I can feel a true genuine smile grow on my face and fill the rest of the room with joy.

"I'm working on being okay now." I gently break away from Kaleb and walk over to the window in the kitchen that faces the backyard.

Out of the corner of my eye I see a small body running into view. He's jumping around in joy asking if we can have a duck pond back here. I smile and nod my head. He smiles brightly and giggles before he runs toward the woods and his image disappears into thin air.

I promise Porter, someday I'll be happy.

Epilogue

Ten years later

My breath slows as I take a moment to look around the room filled with so many people that love me. That love my family. A smile grows on my face as my body fills with gratitude.

I feel an arm wrap around me. I recognize his touch right away.

Kaleb. I look up at his matured face and growing beard. He leans down and kisses my forehead. I take another moment to look back around the room and notice all of his art covering our walls. Theres many, many paintings of the best parts of that summer and lots of paintings from after as well. However, as if under a spotlight the painting he gave me for my birthday is in the center of the room, right above the fireplace mantel. I breathe in, smile and feel all the love surrounding me in this moment.

"How lucky we are." As always, his voice calms me, and I lean into his side. We stand there for a moment admiring the view when there's a knock at the door. I break away from Kaleb and I open the front door to a grinning Joe.

"Hi, sweetheart." Joe leans into a hug and then kisses me on the cheek. "You look beautiful today, as always." I smile at him as he walks through the door and announces himself to the room by saying. "Now where is the birthday boy?"

I hear little feet slap the ground in haste and turn just in time to see the smile on his face as he runs toward Joe.

"Grandpa!!" His little voice screams in joy as he runs into Joe's arms. I look at Kaleb and can tell right away that we're thinking the same thing. How much we love our kid.

"Look at you! How old are you now? You're two now, right?" Porter giggles and shakes his head.

"Nooooo. I'm fooww today." He says this and wiggles his little toes. Porter then grabs Joe's hand and drags him into the other room to talk with his uncles, Charlie and Elijah.

I walk back to Kaleb wrapping my arms around his neck and pull him down to me. I kiss him gently and then create a small amount of space between us. Just enough so I can whisper "I love you and I love our life."

I push off of him and he smacks my butt as I walk away. I giggle while walking outside for some fresh air. I breathe in the smell of green that I love and appreciate the beauty in every moment.

I look out at the woods before I make my way back inside. I notice slight movement between the trees and that's when I see him. I see my younger brother's face peeking out from behind one of the trees, a hand raises up and begins to wave to me as if he were saying goodbye. I realize now that he's been with me all along waiting until he knew I'd be okay without him. His image slowly fades into the woods. A single tear falls down my cheek.

I did it Porter. I'm happy.

ACKNOWLEDGMENTS

First, to my beautiful and incredibly talented sister Oriana Gabrielle, thank you for always being a creative inspiration and supporting me through this twelve-year journey of writing this story.

Second to my lovely, kind, and brilliant cousin Nichole, thank you for literally always being only a phone call away, the all-nighters going over my book with me, and no matter what, always being down to help with ideas, plot holes, story ideas. You have no idea what it means to have someone there ready to support me no matter what.

And last but definitely not least, to my superwoman of an editor and writing coach, Ashly Wallace. You are a phenomenal human being filled with encouragement and love for authors like myself and the work itself. I probably could have eventually done this alone; however, the masterpiece that it is, the impactful and powerful story I created, was created with your support backing me the whole way. Without you I wouldn't have become the author I needed to be to finally finish this story, so thank you. Keep writing, and DON'T LOOK BACK! ;)

ABOUT THE AUTHOR

Chloe Taylor was born in Oregon and lived there for most of her childhood with her mother. This is where she first fell in love with writing.

Now that Chloe has realized her lifelong dream of becoming an author she invites readers into a world woven together over years of thoughtful development. Her debut novel Dark Valley Porter stands as a testament to the power of self-belief and the triumph of embracing one's true calling.

Made in United States
Troutdale, OR
08/04/2024